SIR MOSES MONTEFIORE

1784–1885

SIR MOSES MONTEFIORE

1784–1885

by
Myrtle Franklin
with
Michael Bor

Anthony Blond

Produced by
The Peterhouse Press
Vallis House, Wendover

Designed by Valerie Sargent
Typesetting and Reproduction by
Avocet, Aylesbury

Published by
Muller Blond & White Ltd
55–57 Great Ormond Street
London WC1

ISBN 0 85634 179-7

Printed in Great Britain by
Hazell, Watson & Viney Ltd
Aylesbury, Bucks

Dedicated to
my beloved husband in gratitude
for his help and support.
M.F. July 1984

Sir Moses Montefiore
1784–1883

CONTENTS

ACKNOWLEDGEMENTS

Extracts from Queen Victoria's Journal and the Photographs of Queen Victoria and her family outside Windsor Castle and of Sir Moses on entering his one hundredth year are reproduced by gracious permission of Her Majesty the Queen. Copyright reserved.

Other pictures and extracts are by kind permission of
The British Museum
The BBC Picture Library
The Central Archive of the Jewish People, Jerusalem
The City of London Guildhall Library
The Graphic
The Illustrated London News
Jews College, London
The Jewish Museum, London
The Jewish National University Library, Jerusalem
The Montefiore Endowment Committee
The National Portrait Gallery
The Royal Library, Windsor Castle
The Collection of the late Mr. and Mrs. John Sebag-Montefiore
The Sun Alliance
The Trustees of the Tate Gallery
The Times Newspapers
The Collection of Mr. Alfred Rubens
Professor Y. Ben-Arieh
Mr. D. H. Shandel
Professor R. Loewe
Ms. Leorah Kroyanker
Mr. Roger Cowen
Dr. Harold Rose
Professor A. Newman
Mr. Robert Sebag-Montefiore

My warmest thanks to Peter Medcalf, chairman of the Peterhouse Press, originally introduced to me to prepare a catalogue for the Permanent Exhibition of the Life and Work of Sir Moses Montefiore in the Jerusalem Windmill. Peter suggested that with this material we should make a book. I have much appreciated his skill and patience in producing it. Thanks also to members of my own family. It was fun to work with my son-in-law, Michael Bor, who as an historian was able to write this facinating story, and my daughter Veronica Gould for her help in cataloguing the pictures.

FOREWORD

by Myrtle Franklin

The genesis of this book lay in the drawers of a Queen Anne cabinet I inherited from my parents. In a concealed drawer I discovered scrolls and a letter from my father's great-great-uncle Sir Moses Montefiore. In another drawer was the find which brought Moses and Judith Montefiore to life for me; it was a wooden box filled with magic lantern slides revealing the history of this extraordinary man, and his devoted consort.

His Bible, given to him by his mother with her 'kind love' on the occasion of his marriage was plainly in frequent use, as was his Prayer Book. Both were heavily annotated; particularly moving were his notes above the 84th verse of Psalm 99 about his entering the Holy City of Jerusalem, 17 October 1827.

All these formed the basis for a permanent photographic exhibition, proposed by Mayor Teddy Kollek, in the Windmill; that very windmill which Sir Moses had built outside the Old City Walls of Jerusalem, in order that the impoverished Jews might grind their corn more cheaply.

While I was in Jerusalem working on this project I met Professor Malachi Beit Arie, director of the Jewish National University Library. He introduced me to Dr. Nadav, Keeper of the Archives and Manuscripts. There we found a previously unpublished diary of Sir Moses' fourth visit to the Holy Land, written in his own handwriting. This find was totally unexpected as Sir Moses had ordered all his diaries to be burned on his death.

The diary was small, mostly in pencil, with ink blots. Nevertheless, thanks to Leorah Kroyanker's clever transcription I was able to read a vivid account of his travels, his land purchases, his frustrations and his achievements.

These weeks were perhaps, the most innovative and imaginative of Sir Moses' philanthropic ventures in the Holy Land. Working in terrible heat, he wrote in Jaffa on Monday, 27 August, 'I feel the weather most trying – the heat is dreadful. The East is, as far as my experience goes, a hard trial of patience.'

The stories he told in this little notebook and in a diary of his famous mission to the East on behalf of the innocent Jews suffering from the Damascus libel were told so vividly that I was tempted to accept the challenge of working on a book to tell more about the travels and hazards of this remarkable man.

Myrtle Franklin
July 1984

BIBLIOGRAPHY

1 *Sir Moses' diaries for 1840 and 1855* (Archives of the Jewish and National University Library).
2 *'Diaries of Sir Moses and Lady Montefiore'*, edited by Dr. Louis Loewe (1983 edition, The Jewish Historical Society of England, The Jewish Museum).
3 *'Private Journal of a Visit to Egypt and Palestine', 1827,* by Judith Montefiore (1836, London).
4 *'The Damascus Affair.' Diary of Louis Loewe, July–November 1840* (Ramsgate, 1940).
5 *Board of Deputies Minutes, 1840–1846.* (Woburn House).
6 *Notes from a Private Journal of a Visit to Egypt and Palestine, 1839,* by Judith Montefiore (1885, London).
7 *The Jewish Manual,* edited by Lady Montefiore (1846) (1983 edition, New York).
8 *'Diary of a Tour to Jerusalem and Alexandria in 1855 with Sir Moses and Lady Montefiore'* by Mrs. H. Guedalla (1890, London).
9 *'Sir Moses Montefiore: A Centennial Biography'*, by Lucien Wolf (1884, London).
10 *'Internationales Montefiore Album'*, edited by Dr. Joseph Fiebermann (Frankfurt, 1885).
11 *Sir Moses' obituary,* The Times, Wednesday, July 29th 1885.
12 *'Moses Montefiore'* by Paul Goodman (1925, The Jewish Publication Society of America, Philadelphia).
13 *'Three Centuries of Anglo–Jewish History'*, edited by V. D. Lipman (1961, The Jewish Historical Society of England).
14 *'Sir Moses Montefiore: A life in the service of Jewry'*, by Dr. S. U. Nahon, (1965, Bureau for Jewish Communities and Organizations of the Jewish Agency).
15 *'The Life and Times of Sir Moses Montefiore'* by Lionel Kochan, History Today, January 1973.
16 *Imperial Continental Gas Association 1824–1974*, 150th anniversary, Westerham Press Ltd, (1974).
17 *'Napoleon and the Jews'*, by Franz Kobler (1975, Massada Press, Jerusalem).
18 *'Revolutionary Jews: From Marx to Trotsky'*, by Robert S. Wistrich (1976, London).
19 *'The Course of Modern Jewish History'*, by Howard Morley Sachar (1977 edition, New York).
20 *'The Rediscovery of the Holy Land in the Nineteenth Century'*, by Yehoshua Ben-Arieh (1979, The Magnes Press, The Hebrew University Jerusalem).
21 *'Sir Moses Montefiore: A Symposium'*, edited by V. D. Lipman, (1982, The Oxford Centre for Postgraduate Hebrew Studies and the Jewish Historical Society of England).
22 *'Doctors Afield: Dr. Thomas Hodgkin's Friendship with Sir Moses Montefiore'*, by Amalie M. Cass, (Massachusetts Medical Society) The New England Journal of Medicine, No. 310, pp. 401–404, February, 1984.
23 An essay on 'Dr Louis Loewe', by Professor Raphael Loewe, to be published in a collection of essays, edited by V. D. Lipman, by Oxford University Press in 1985.

INTRODUCTION

by Aubrey Newman, MA, DPhil, FRHistS

The life of Sir Moses Montefiore spanned à century of Anglo-Jewish life, but there is a much deeper significance than merely a hundred years of service. The Anglo-Jewish community of the late eighteenth century was vastly different from that of the late nineteenth; it differed in size, in the range of its activities, in the extent to which it had become accepted within the non-Jewish 'host' community around it. Sir Moses was to a considerable extent linked with all of these changes, and indeed to some degree he presided over them. But there is a greater importance to him even than that. To many people throughout the world Sir Moses came to represent Anglo-Jewry, indeed even Jewry itself. He became, consciously or sub-consciously, a roving ambassador for world Jewry, so that vast areas of the world which he had never seen, and which indeed were largely unknown to the European world at the time of his birth, looked with respect on him. Australia and New Zealand joined the Far West of the North American continent in the ceremonies to mark his hundredth birthday and to lament his death. Synagogues and hospitals were named after him; Lodges of Freemasons and associations of various friendly societies took his name to pay him honour; and sovereigns from very many different countries paid tribute to him. All over the world too Jewish communities in distress turned to him for support, and that support was never denied.

In his origins Moses Montefiore was typical of many of the Jews of the late eighteenth-century Anglo-Jewry. His parents were Sephardim from Italy who had come to Britain but who had retained close links with their native Leghorn, so that it is not really surprising that Moses should have been born there. Educated in London, however, and apprenticed to trade there, he became part of the contemporary scene, both as a member of the Bevis Marks community of Sephardi Jews and as a part of the non-Jewish environment. He was a member of the Surrey militia, a member of a freemasons' lodge, but a member too of such an essential body in his own synagogue as the *Lavadores*, those who were responsible for the last care of the dead. His business career was largely in the field of finance, and his links with the Mocatta and Rothschild families undoubtedly made it possible for him to retire from active business life in his early thirties, thus giving him an opportunity for a public career on the grand scale, a career in which his wife Judith was a full participant and source of encouragement.

What is untypical of his career, however, is the way in which he was able to secure recognition both from his fellow-citizens and his co-religionists at a time when those two terms were hardly likely to be over-lapping. There was no full political 'emancipation' for Jews in Britain during most of his life; indeed it could be argued that as Jews were not yet permitted to sit in the House of Lords – an event which occurred just before his death – there was no full emancipation until after he died. Yet he gained many public honours – including the grant of a baronetcy – and indeed was given those honours by the non-Jewish world as much for his advocacy of the cause of his suffering co-religionists as for any other reason. In support of oppressed Jews he travelled all over Europe, visits which were almost always at a considerable inconvenience and often at very real risk of life. When he was eighty-seven, the British government had great difficulty in persuading him not to make a journey to Persia; instead, he journeyed to Russia where he interviewed the Tsar. His visits to the Holy Land and the work he did there were of course vital for the future development of Jewish settlement, while Yemin Moshe remains a monument of his vision of the need for settlement outside the Old City of Jerusalem.

By the time of his death, Anglo-Jewry had become enlarged over ten-fold, and the nature of Anglo-Jewry had been transformed as a result of migrations from Russia. Still he remained in effect 'a Prince of the Dispersion' and still he was regarded as virtually 'the Grand Old Man' of Jewry. It was not merely a result of sheer survival; it was a genuine respect for a man who had never spared himself for his fellow Jews, and had always in consequence inspired genuine sympathy amongst non-Jews for his fellow-Jews.

The calendar has brought round the double centenaries, the celebration of the two hundredth anniversary of his birth and the commemoration of the hundredth anniversary of his death. This volume marks both, and will enable a wider circle to understand something of what Sir Moses came to represent to his contemporaries, his co-religionists, and his family.

The book owes a great deal indeed to his (collateral) descendants, to the pride which they rightly feel in his achievements, and to their laudable desire to share those sentiments to the wider world. Above all it owes a great deal to Myrtle Franklin who inspired it and all those who have contributed to it.

Aubrey Newman

1. FAMILY, EARLY LIFE AND MARRIAGE

Sir Moses Montefiore was born in 1784 and lived to be one hundred. He was four when the Bastille was being stormed and the French Revolution was beginning. He came of age the year which witnessed the victory of Trafalgar, and as a young man met Nelson and Lady Hamilton at a dinner party.

He was to achieve a unique place in Anglo Jewish history. At the age of forty he had already amassed a fortune, and retired from full time business life to devote the next fifty years to taking an active and successful part in securing the civil liberties and general welfare of the Jews throughout the world, interviewing kings, queens, sultans and czars in many capitals on their behalf.

In 1784 his father was on a business trip to Italy and his mother, although eight months pregnant, determined to travel with him, so Sir Moses was born on the 24 October in Leghorn, Italy, at the house owned by Moses Haim Racah, who was Sir Moses' great uncle and godfather.

Montefiores had been living in Italy from the sixteenth century in Pesaro. The earliest proof is a curtain for the Holy Ark of the Pesaro Synagogue, embroidered by Rachel (née Olivetti) in 1630 in honour of her husband Yehuda Montefiore. It is now in the Italian Synagogue in Jerusalem.

Sir Moses' grandfather was Moses Haim Vita Montefiore (1712–89), whose mother was related to Sir Solomon de Medina, the first professing Jew to be knighted in England after making a large fortune financing the Duke of Marlborough's campaigns. Moses Haim was a merchant who married Esther Racah (1735–1812) in Leghorn, settled in England in 1758 and had nine sons and eight daughters. He had laid the basis of the family fortunes and cemented the associations which brought the rise of the Montefiores to distinction in

Moses Racah of Leghorn, Godfather and Great Uncle of Sir Moses.

The Montefiore Parochet embroidered in Pesaro in 1620 by an ancestress of Sir Moses.

Portrait of Moses Montefiore's mother.

England. This was particularly enhanced in the congregation of Sephardi (Spanish and Portuguese) Jews in London centred at the Bevis Marks synagogue. A highly cultured, influential and wealthy Jewish community emerged.

The mother of Sir Moses was Rachel Lumbroso de Mattos Mocatta (1762–1841), daughter of Abraham Mocatta, a Jewish broker. The Mocattas, like the Montefiores, had been living in Italy in the sixteenth century and from Venice they emigrated to Holland to trade. When William of Orange entered England in 1688, more Dutch Jews were invited, including the Mocattas. By 1694 Isaac de Mocatta had created a firm, which became Mocatta and Keysers in the 1730s, and 'Goldsmid and Mocatta', bullion brokers to the Bank of England and the East India Company, by 1783. Moses Mocatta (1768–1857) was responsible for superintending young Moses' studies in Hebrew, and instilled in his young protegé his own enthusiasm for the traditions and fortunes of Jews and Judaism. The young Moses would go every Sunday for his religious instruction, and took his younger brother Abraham, although the latter was not so enthusiastic. Mocatta had translated Isaac Troki's *The Strengthening of the Faith*, the title of which might be applicable to his nephew's lifetime activities.

Sir Moses' favourite uncle was Joshua, a swashbuckling soldier who began as a lawyer. From 1791 Joshua went on an expedition to take possession of the island of Bulama off west Africa. It was a disastrous expedition; he was one of the few survivors to return. He wrote an account of his adventures, of how he hoisted the British flag at Bulama and organised the economy of the colony. He travelled to Sierra Leone and entered the army, claimed he was the first Jew to hold a military commission in Britain, served in various parts of the world, and in 1809, as an officer in the York Light Infantry, was at the taking of Martinique and Guadaloupe. He retired in America, again practised as a lawyer and published a weekly political journal *Men and Measures*. He married a second time at the age of 73 and died in Vermont in 1843 aged 81, leaving seven children, the youngest of whom was only six weeks old! Sir Moses retained vivid recollections of his 'Uncle Josh', whose laced red coat, cocked hat and sword and fund of anecdotes, and his life as a practising Jew, appealed greatly to his nephew.

Moses' parents lived at No. 3, Kennington Terrace, Vauxhall. His father had a business in Italian goods, especially Leghorn straw bonnets and Carrara marbles. Moses was the first of eight children; there were two more sons, Abraham and Horatio, and five daughters, Sarah, Esther, Abigail, Rebecca and Justina. Marriages linked them with other leading Jewish families. Abraham's second marriage was to Henrietta Rothschild (sister of Nathan Mayer Rothschild) and Horatio married Sarah, a daughter of David Mocatta. Of the daughters, Sarah married Solomon Sebag and was the mother of Joseph Sebag who, after Sir Moses' death, took the name of Montefiore; Abigail married Benjamin Gompertz, the mathematician; Rebecca married Joseph Solomons, Justina married Benjamin Cohen, Judith Montefiore's brother; and Esther died in a fire in the house when she was only fifteen. Sir Moses' father never recovered from that tragedy.

According to his mother, Moses was a beautiful, strong and very tall child. He went to school in Kennington where he was renowned for copying short moral epigrams from books. This became a life-time habit in his diaries, which contained at the beginning or end of the day's activities some poetry referring to moral or literary subjects or quotations from famous authors.

House at Leghorn in which Sir
Moses was born.

In his 1829 diaries, one can glean these epigrammatic quotations:
'Be content with what God has allotted you, and you are rich.'
'To learn, listen. To be safe, be silent.'
'No man can be happy who does not devote at least five or six hours daily to some useful employment.'
He acted on these maxims throughout his life.

From his schooldays Sir Moses learnt and exhibited his respect for established authorities. He regarded this as a sacred duty, and henceforth in public or private he would only accept the decision of an acknowledged authority. He left school at thirteen, and since Jews could not study for the professions or the law, his father apprenticed him with a neighbour of his, Mr. Robert Johnson, a wholesale tea merchant and grocer in Eastcheap. Whatever the weather, young Moses walked to the city and back home every day. In his first commercial experience he worked diligently and learnt to keep a strict account of his own expenses. Then, in 1804, his uncle, Moses Mocatta, purchased for him for £1,200 the right to practise as one of the twelve Jewish brokers licensed by the City. Through Mocatta and Goldsmid he had become a broker. In Asher Goldsmid's house in Morden he was to meet Lord Nelson and befriend Goldsmid's son, Isaac Lyon Goldsmid, the financier and philanthropist, who supported Negro and Jewish Emancipation, the restriction of capital punishment, and was a propagandist for popular education. Sir Moses developed similar interests.

In 1809 Sir Moses exhibited his combined loyalty to Judaism and devotion to Britain by volunteering for the local Militia. He always maintained that Jews should be loyal and patriotic to their government. From 1810 to 1814 he was a Captain of the Surrey Militia, which meant serving for 30 to 40 days each year and learning the bugle and French. He cut a handsome figure in uniform. Six foot three and with a robust voice, young Moses had 'presence'. During this time in 1812 he was made a Freemason, joining the Moira Lodge. He resigned from this in 1819 becoming an honorary member. The Lodge was named after him in 1864 but he was never an active member. Eighteen twelve was a crucial year in his life for two other reasons. His connections with Nathan Mayer Rothschild, the boldest speculator and shrewdest financier of the age, began. Moses became intimately associated with Rothschild's enterprises and acted as his stockbroker. In 1806, Rothschild had married Hannah Cohen, and, on 10 June 1812, Moses married Hannah's sister, Judith. Their father, Levi Barent Cohen (1740–1808), was a wealthy merchant from Amsterdam who had settled in England.

Moses' marriage to Judith was the most important event in his life. The marriage linked Sephardi and Ashkenazi and it remained an axiom of his life that there were no real differences between Jews. The date of the marriage was commemorated by him whenever possible (by the laying of foundation stones for synagogues or charitable institutions) to unite every important activity in his life with his marriage. In memory of that day, he treasured the prayer-shawl which had been held over them during the marriage ceremony and prayers, and it was placed over his head at his death. Judith was a strict adherent of Judaism. They never neglected to light the Sabbath lamp; she could read and translate Hebrew, and spoke French, German and Italian fluently. Her idealism and commitment to Judaism had an inestimable influence on her husband. They shared the devoted care in the observance of the practices and customs of their religion, and she became the inspiration behind his bold and perspicacious missions that made him a major figure in

Moses Montefiore as a captain in the Surrey Militia.

16

Stormy sea outside Ramsgate Harbour.

Judith Montefiore at the time of her marriage.

Moses Montefiore caricature from an etching 1818.

Sir Moses' Coat of Arms.

East Cliff Lodge, Ramsgate, Kent.

Judith and Moses Montefiore at the time of their marriage.

אשא עיני א ההרים מאין יבוא עזרי
עזרי מעם ה'

The ancient coat of arms of the Montefiore family.

Jewish history rather than merely a wealthy financier. They inspired each other, and shared all the risks and dramas in travelling abroad.

The marriage was remarkably harmonious, as is apparent from their private diaries, with the countless expressions of veneration and affection for each other. A unity in their sense of duty and moral purpose was provided by their orthodox Judaism—daily prayers, participation in services in synagogue, respect for dietary laws, and abstention from work on the Sabbath and for religious festivals. This applied under the most difficult circumstances during their numerous travels abroad. They lived the Jewish way, and always referred to the association of prosperity with the blessing of God. Moses ascribed his success to the wisdom of her advice and her sympathy with his activities. Their ideals blended for 50 years. They also became a centre for Jewish philanthropic activities in London, her humanitarian instincts combining with his, and being his companion in nearly all his endeavours. She accompanied him in all his foreign missions until 1859 and supplemented his work abroad.

They both expressed their views on their marriage. In the 1870s, Sir Moses looked back on his achievements and thanked his wife:

'I am no great man. The little good that I have accomplished, or rather that I intended to accomplish, I am indebted for it to my never-to-be-forgotten wife, whose enthusiasm for everything that is noble and whose religiousness sustained me in my career.'

Two days after their marriage, she wrote on the essence of her attraction to him:

'I do not know any circumstances more pleasing to me than to perceive that my dear Monte is religiously inclined. It is that sort of religion which he possesses that in my opinion is most essential—a fellow feeling and benevolence.'

She re-read this diary in December 1825 and remarked:

'On perusing the few preceding pages, written during the first month of my marriage, I could not restrain my tears produced from a variety of feelings of joy and sorrow, joy in possessing in health and prosperity the good and worthy husband of my choice.'

and sorrow that they could not have children. This was probably because of the fall over a staircase railing two storeys high into the hall below which she sustained as a child. Caring for Jews throughout the world became the magnificent substitute.

The original coat of arms of the Montefiore family was appropriate to the lives which Moses and Judith were to lead. The mottoes on it were 'Be strong as a lion to perform the will of thy Father in Heaven'; 'When I lift up mine eyes unto the hills (I ask) whence cometh my help? My help cometh from the Eternal'; 'The righteous shall flourish like a palm tree; he shall grow like a cedar in Lebanon.' Moses merely simplified the inscriptions to 'Jerusalem' and 'Think and Thank'. Throughout their 50 years together the place where they retreated to 'think and thank', their favourite quiet haunt, was Smithambottom in Surrey. There they enjoyed a complete rest from their travels abroad and stress of London life. They used to go on Sundays and sometimes remain until the middle of the week, walking over hills, imbibing their favourite beverage, wine, and staying at the local inn 'The Red Lion'. Their last visit was in June 1861. Sir Moses then explained its significance:

'Smithambottom appears to me to be the same quiet place it was half-a-century ago. It was ever to me a caution against ambition, and has led me to esteem independence far beyond riches. At this place, man appeared to want but little. With peace and content, and the quietness of the place, which afforded us the opportunity of keeping the Sabbaths undisturbed by the fluctuations which were at that period daily taking place in London from the vicissitudes of the war, endeared Smithambottom to my dear Judith and myself

17

Hazards of travel—highwaymen.

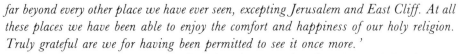

far beyond every other place we have ever seen, excepting Jerusalem and East Cliff. At all these places we have been able to enjoy the comfort and happiness of our holy religion. Truly grateful are we for having been permitted to see it once more.'

After his wife's death, it was in Smithambottom that he planned the College that was to be named after her. He wrote on 25 September 1864:

'I hope that, by Divine blessing, I have been of some use to my fellow-creatures, both Jews and Christians, and I believe I may add, "Moors". To God alone, who helped and sustained me, be honour and glory. I believe that my dear Judith would have approved my conduct. My angel guide of so many happy years being no longer with me on earth in mortal form, I sincerely pray the God of Israel to be my guide, and to permit her heavenly spirit to comfort me, and keep me in the right path. A visit to Smithambottom is now to me very similar to that of the solemn "Day of Atonement", with the exception of fasting. I hope hours spent in serious reflection on the past incidents of a long life tend to make me better, and constitute a great moral lesson.'

The Montefiores had been inseparable, affectionate, and loyal as the Queen and the Prince Consort.

The Montefiores' first residence was No. 4, New Court, St. Swithin's Lane. Their neighbours were Nathan M. Rothschild and his wife, Judith's sister. Around the dinner table of the Rothschilds sat the most important personalities of politics, finance and diplomacy. The Montefiores also frequently visited the Rothschilds' country house in Highgate, their brother-in-law, S. M. Samuel's summer residence in Hastings, and Moses' mother at Kennington Terrace. They studied French in the evenings and, before their first journey to Jerusalem in 1827, had travelled four times to France and Italy and twice to Belgium and Germany. On their first visit to France in 1816 they bought their carriage in Paris from the famous coach builder Beaupré and stayed with Solomon de Rothschild. In 1817 they bought Tinley Lodge farm and in 1822 rented East Cliff Lodge, Ramsgate for a year.

On 28 August 1824, Moses' brother Abraham died. Within a year Moses had retired from full-time business activities. 'Thank God, and be content' responded his wife. Henceforth, they dedicated most of their energies, time, and assets to social and philanthropic work. They moved from New Court to 35, Park Lane, their permanent London home. Later the number changed to 99, Park Lane, although he headed his London address notepaper 'Grosvenor Gate'. There he formulated his belief in the efficacy of philanthropy and

The President of Israel, Chaim Hertzog, unveiling the plaque to Sir Moses at his old home at 99 Park Lane, London on 28 March 1984.

New Court 1824.

18

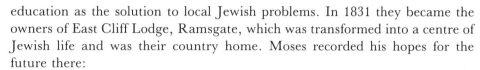

Queen Victoria with her family, Windsor Castle 1857.

Testimonial to Sir Moses and Lady Montefiore by the son of the Viceroy of Egypt.

education as the solution to local Jewish problems. In 1831 they became the owners of East Cliff Lodge, Ramsgate, which was transformed into a centre of Jewish life and was their country home. Moses recorded his hopes for the future there:

> *'May the Almighty bless and preserve my dear Judith and myself to enjoy the possession of it for many years, that we may also have the happiness of seeing our intended synagogue completed, and always have a large congregation.'*

A cousin, David Mocatta, was the architect who submitted drawings for the synagogue and the excavations of the foundation walls were completed by 29 July. The dedication of the synagogue on 16 June 1833 was made the occasion of a festive reunion of English Jewry. Moses became a prominent figure in Ramsgate. Adjacent were grounds owned by the Duchess of Kent and in September 1835, when Princess Victoria was visiting Ramsgate, he gave them a golden key to the gate which separated the residences so that they could walk through his grounds when they wished.

Moses had an abiding reverence for royalty and a close association with Queen Victoria. The Montefiores dined with Princess Victoria in 1836, often attended the Queen's drawing room, were invited to Her Majesty's State Ball at Buckingham Palace in 1844, and took the young Prince Toussoun, son of the Pasha of Egypt, to Windsor Castle in 1858 to meet the Queen and the Prince Consort. Sir Moses expressed his veneration:

> *'I never in my life witnessed a more lovely picture than the Queen, the Prince Consort and the Royal children, beauty and goodness combined, a perfect picture of a noble family.'*

After Toussoun Pasha's second reception by the Queen the following year, Sir Moses was convinced that friendly relations between England and Egypt would be preserved, and when the Prince Consort died in 1861 he praised him not only for his amiability and benevolence but because he was liberal as regards religious freedom to all.

The Montefiores had their share of hazards to overcome in England. In 1836 they were in a vessel, the *Magnet*, off Margate and in thick fog hit a sandbank. Later a steamer, the *Red Rover*, struck their bow and sank. Its passengers and crew clambered on to the *Magnet* which, severely damaged, managed to reach the shore:

> *'My poor dear wife conducted herself with her usual admirable courage. We were, in all probability, never in our lives in more imminent danger. God be praised for His great mercy for granting us His protection.'*

A year later, someone fired a pistol at them when they were travelling in their carriage, near Welling, on the road from Rochester to London. In April 1838, Lady Montefiore was on her own in the carriage, visiting her sister Hannah de Rothschild, when the horses were frightened, broke free of the harness and damaged the carriage considerably. Ten years later, while at a soirée at the Marquis of Salisbury's, thieves ransacked their house in Park Lane and stole gold, silver and valuable mementoes. Yet, compared with some of the dangers and escapes shared on their travels abroad, these incidents in England paled into insignificance.

Sir Moses regularly penned his thanks to his wife for her constant support:

'To Lady Montefiore, I owe a debt of gratitude; her counsels and zeal for our religion and love to our brethren were at all times conspicuous. They animated me under difficulties and consoled me under disappointments.'

On the anniversary of their marriage in 1844 he celebrated:

'Thirty-two years have passed since the Almighty God of Israel, in His great goodness, blessed me with my dear Judith, and for ever shall I be most truly grateful for this blessing, the great cause of my happiness through life. From the first day of our happy union to this hour I have had every reason for increased love and esteem, and truly may I say, each succeeding year has brought with it greater proofs of her admirable character. A better and kinder wife never existed.'

They shared the Victorian virtues of charity, industry, discipline and self-help, and comforted each other in sickness as in health. Judith was ill on nearly every journey abroad, and her husband cared for her diligently, always breaking the travelling to give her time to recover. When *he* suffered from a severe illness for several months in 1834 she rarely left his bedside day or night, except to snatch a few hours sleep. Twenty years later, Sir Moses was again very ill and confined to his bed for 43 days. Judith wrote to a close friend on 5 March 1854:

'He has suffered severely, and been in danger, but now I trust, with the Almighty's blessing, that he will progress towards recovery.'

An eminent physician examined his heart and lungs. The prognosis was pessimistic; heart feeble, poison in his blood, digestive organs impaired—and this was 30 years before his death!

Marriage sustained the Montefiores for fifty years in an idyllic union.

The Montefiores on the terrace of their Ramsgate villa, East Cliff Lodge.

East Cliff Lodge when it was purchased by the Montefiores.

2. CITY AND POLITICAL ACTIVITIES

When Sir Moses began his career as one of the twelve Jewish brokers licensed by the City, Nathan M. Rothschild was guaranteeing the payment of bullion to Wellesley's troops. By 1815 Rothschild had reaped enormous profits from the allied state loans he had floated and his credit system, founded upon an intricate intelligence network, won the confidence of European rulers. In 1813 he had brought out the British loan for £12 million for military operations against Napoleon, and Moses and his brother, Abraham, as Montefiore Bros. were henceforth associated as brokers with the transactions of the house of Rothschild. With war in Europe and frenetic activity on the Stock Exchange, Moses was in constant contact with N. M. Rothschild, whose judicious recommendations regarding the bullion market and foreign exchanges enabled him to avoid hazardous monetary transactions. At No. 2, New Court, Rothschild organised a unique news service via couriers, who arrived at all hours of the day or night with despatches from the continent. Carrier pigeons were also employed, and Sir Moses recalled how he was roused at 5 a.m. to hear the news of Napoleon's escape from Elba. Rothschild rode to Downing Street to communicate the information to the government.

This was a crucial relationship, because in 1806 Sir Moses was defrauded of £30,000. He never forget that day, 20 August, but who was responsible?

"N.N." robbed me of all and more than I had. Blessed be the Almighty that He has not suffered my enemies to triumph over me.' (20 August 1823, Sir Moses' Diary.)
'This day, 20th August, five and twenty years ago, in 1806, "J.E.D." (Daniels) robbed me of all I possessed in the world, and left me deeply in debt; but it pleased the Almighty in His great mercy to enable me in the course of a few years to pay everyone who had been a sufferer through me to the full extent of their loss.' (20 August 1831, Sir Moses' Diary.)

Nathan Mayer Rothschild.

Despite this early setback, Moses became rapidly recognised for his straightforward dealing, perspicacity, courteous manners and amiable disposition. His enterprise and steadiness gave clients confidence; he began the publication of a weekly price-list of stocks quoted on the Exchange, became renowned for his scrupulous honesty in his transactions and was entrusted with huge amounts of money for charities and for the Holy Land.

Moses' diaries on his business years are crammed with references to rumours of war, the health of kings and emperors, governments' policies, house calls on royalty and cabinet members, and entries on international politics and conflicts between nations. These events were vital to investment bankers' loans. His last major business transaction was the most significant, in 1835, the successful contracting of the £20 million loan by Rothschild and Montefiore for the compensation to owners of freed slaves, enabling the British Government to carry the Slave Emancipation Act into effect.

Moses was punctilious in his respect for authority and governments, irrespective of the ideological orientation of the régime in power. He was energetic in his business years. He created the Alliance Assurance Company in 1824, with N. M. Rothschild, Benjamin Gompertz and Samuel Gurney. Montefiore remained actively interested in the affairs of the Company until his death 60 years later. The Company is still prospering now under the name Sun Alliance Insurance Group. He was an innovator in the Imperial Continental Gas Association, the first to introduce street gas-lighting to European cities. It won him election to the Royal Society in 1836 for the technical innovations of the Company, 'as a gentleman much attached to science and its practical use'. He frequently inspected the Company's continental establishments, was advised to terminate it but declined, and was rewarded for his enterprise and courage. He studied the history of insurance and was elected President for life by both these Companies. Directors and shareholders appreciated his sound judgement, caution, and energy in the promotion and welfare of their affairs.

The emergence of the Imperial Continental Gas Association reveals a typical example of nineteenth century British commercial enterprise and initiative. It was conceived by Major General Sir William Congreve who formed the Company in December 1824 solely to introduce gas lighting to European towns and cities. He approached Moses Montefiore, Matthias Attwood and I. L. Goldsmid to provide the necessary funds to float a company, and despite financially shaky beginnings, their optimism and sense of adventure carried them through. Their first successes in public lighting by gas were in Ghent, Rotterdam, Hanover and Berlin and, by 1828, the Association was supplying 6,000 lights from these four undertakings on the continent. There were no profits yet, and it was not until 1832 that the first dividend was paid. The Association then entered a period of expansion into other major European cities and towns, and developed gas lighting in theatres, private homes, factories and railway stations, particularly the main termini. Sir Moses played a significant rôle in this remarkable achievement of a British company, predominantly British-owned and financed, which had captured a huge share of the continental market, consolidated existing contracts and by 1850 owned sixteen profitable undertakings in five countries. Despite European wars and competition from rival companies the Association flourished so that by 1875 over one million lights were being supplied on the continent by the Company.

In 1825 Moses branched out into banking with the Provincial Bank of Ireland, issued the first notes over the counter of its Dublin offices, and as Director attended regularly. He was now involved with eight companies (Alliance Assurance, Alliance Marine Assurance, Imperial Continental Gas, Provincial Bank of Ireland, Imperial Brazilian Mining, Chilean and Peruvian Mining, the Irish Manufactory, and the British Colonial Silk Company), and later became a director of the South Eastern Railway Company, with a gold pass. The silk industry was a major interest throughout his travelling. Abroad he attended meetings and organised dinners for the Company and was constantly interested in the production of silk wherever it was grown, encouraging the planting of mulberry trees in the Holy Land. As an authority in the financial world he was offered many other directorships but declined, including those of the Panama Canal and Suez Canal Companies. Eighteen twenty-five witnessed his withdrawal from full-time involvement in the excited state of affairs of the financial world, although he maintained an active interest and participation in the administration of his holdings and of the Companies.

On 16 May 1831 he signed over his Stock Exchange licence to his brother, Horatio, although he still had his anxieties as a director of the Provincial Bank of Ireland during the 1857 financial crisis. He was inspecting the Gas Company in Belgium and attending Board meetings of the Alliance Life and Fire Insurance Company and the Imperial Continental Gas Company into his eighties. The Alliance declared on his hundredth birthday:

'Among the business undertakings which Sir Moses during his long and useful life has assisted in prompting, none is more prosperous or more deeply indebted to his sagacity and judgement than the Alliance Office.'

The 25,000 English Jews in 1815 had participated effectively in the war effort against Napoleon and were slowly consolidating their liberties. In England, Jewish emancipation was a gradual process, and Moses preferred it that way. In 1820 he went frequently to the two Houses to watch the progress of the Jews Emancipation Bill and had no intention of intervening on the grand scale:

'I am an enemy of all sudden transitions. The Jew must, in his claims and wishes, not outstrip his age. Let him advance slowly but steadily; let him gradually accustom his Christian fellow-citizens to his gradual progress and success in public life.'

This approach seemed justified until 1828, when the repeal of the Test and Corporation Acts allowed Catholics and Nonconformists to sit as MPs. Jews could legally be elected to Parliament but could not in practice take their seats because the swearing-in formula included 'as a true Christian'. They could not hold any civil or military office under the Crown or in municipal councils or the law or university. The Rothschilds, Goldsmids, Cohens, and Montefiores began to campaign for full political and civil rights for Jews, and as members of the British upper class these families had a crucial rôle to play.

Moses' representative career began with his appointment to the British Board of Deputies in 1828, which held regular meetings only in the 1830s. This was to become the springboard of his unique position in the history of Anglo-Jewry. He was henceforth involved in every major event in Jewish history in his time, and immediately engaged in the struggle for Jewish emancipation, alongside N. M. Rothschild, Sir I. L. Goldsmid and the Duke of Sussex, uncle of Queen Victoria. The 'struggle', for Moses, warranted cautious tactics in discussions with ministers, peers and MPs. The first ventures included a meeting, in June 1828, for I. L. Goldsmid and Moses with Catholics and Dissenters on the best mode of obtaining civil equality for Jews. Frequent dinners, entertainments and meetings were held at the Rothschilds in early 1829 to discuss religious and civil liberties with politicians and the nobility.

In his diaries for 1829 and 1830 Moses made numerous references to meetings and delegations on behalf of a Bill to remove Jewish disabilities. In February 1829, he and N. M. Rothschild saw Sir James Mackintosh about promoting a Bill to allow Jews to hold freehold land; in March, he met Daniel O'Connell and Dr. Hume and others to discuss the issues of Jewish emancipation. He was at the Rothschilds when the petition for both Houses was read, and the same day at a meeting of deputies from the London synagogues at the Mocattas' home. In April we find Moses and N. M. Rothschild with the Lord Chancellor at the House of Lords; a meeting of Montefiore, Rothschild, I. L. Goldsmid and Moses Mocatta resolved that John M. Pearce should prepare a petition for Jews to be admitted to Parliament. They consulted Lord Brougham and Lord Bexley. Ironically, the very next day, a Jew was presented by the Duke of Norfolk to King William IV at a dance given by His Majesty at St. James' Palace. It was Moses Montefiore, the first Jew to be so honoured. One day later, he recorded that Lord Bexley recommended Sir Thomas Baring to bring the Jewish Emancipation Bill before the House of Commons. The next month, he was at the Mocattas' residence for a meeting of the Deputies, the petition was accepted in its final form. He, Rothschild, and Goldsmid took it to Lord Bexley, who remarked that the Duke of Wellington would oppose it that year, yet, at a dinner with numerous Lords at the Rothschilds, Moses found them in support of the petition.

The campaign continued throughout 1830. In January, a deputation to the

Sir Robert Peel and the Duke of Wellington.

Sir Moses in the uniform of a sheriff of London.

Duke of Sussex was prepared, and another meeting of the Deputies at the Mocattas' resolved to meet the Duke of Wellington, who, too absorbed in party political issues in the Commons, advised them to defer their application to Parliament. On 22 February a Bill was presented in the Commons by Robert Grant, but Moses counselled that Jews should not insist at this stage on obtaining the privilege of sitting as MPs. On 16 April, a Commons' debate for repeal of civil disabilities won a vote of 115 to 97 but the opposition rallied and on a further reading the Bill was defeated by 228 to 165 votes. By November, petitions had been prepared for both Houses and Moses signed them, but within six months the Jewish Relief Bill had been postponed. A year on, in June 1833, he asked G. R. Dawson to intercede with his brother-in-law, Sir Robert Peel, to withdraw his opposition to the Jewish Emancipation Bill. However, a Bill carried in the Commons was thrown out by the Lords by a majority of 50; a similar Bill in 1834 was thrown out by 92 votes.

The watershed was in 1835. By the Sheriffs' Declaration Bill, a Jew could at last enter the office of Sheriff, the first political office to which a Jew was elected. David Salomons had been elected for London and Middlesex; now he did not have to violate his own religious convictions. Moses Montefiore had also been collecting honours. In 1830 he was elected a member of the Athenaeum. In 1835 he was elected a member of the Merchant Taylors Company (the first Jew to be granted this) and made President of the London Committee of Deputies of British Jews, and in 1837 Sheriff of London and Middlesex. As President *and* Sheriff he became the most prominent member of the Anglo-Jewish community. He remodelled the Deputies' constitution so that it became the mouthpiece of British Jews, monitoring the progress of legislation to safeguard Jewish interests and considering all appeals from foreign brethren. The Board became the sole means of communication between Anglo-Jewry and the Government. Sir Moses himself nurtured most of the contacts with ministers and received official despatches from the Foreign Office. He imprinted his own style of Jewish diplomacy—lobbies in Parliament, letters to editors and 'good will' negotiations to change Government policies.

As Sheriff of London and Middlesex, he achieved a unique position in the non-Jewish world. He had been doubtful about accepting the Shrievalty because he maintained his personal religious practices and therefore would not be able to attend church ceremonies and, at official banquets, would have to be allowed to bring from his home his dishes, cutlery and meat. Nevertheless, proposed by T. A. Curtis, Governor of the Bank of England, he was unanimously elected Sheriff on 24 June 1836, and judged it an honour to all Jews, despite foreseeing further obstacles:

Below Left. *The procession of the sheriffs of London 1847.*

Below Right. *The procession of H.M. Queen Victoria to Guildhall 1837, passing through Trafalgar Square.*

*'I shall have the greatest difficulties to contend with in the execution of my duty; diffi-
culties which I shall meet with at the very outset. The day I enter on my office is the
commencement of our New Year. I shall therefore have to walk to Westminster instead of
going in my state carriage, nor, I fear, shall I be able to dine with my friends at the
inauguration dinner which, from time immemorial, is given on the 30th September. I
shall, however, endeavour to persuade my colleagues to change the day to the 5th of
October.'*

He succeeded in persuading his colleagues. The inauguration dinner on the 5th
was followed on the 11th by another of equal significance for him:

*'To West Cliff, where I had the honour of dining with their Royal Highnesses, the
Duchess of Kent and the Princess Victoria. There were 13 at table, and it was impossible
for it to have been more agreeable. I returned home quite enraptured with the very kind and
obliging manner in which I had been distinguished by Her Royal Highness.'*

In July 1837, as Sheriff-elect, he presented an address of homage to Queen
Victoria the year of her Coronation, and the Montefiores attended the first
court reception of the new Queen.

For the next year he was totally occupied with duties as the Sheriff. In his
inauguration speech at the Merchant Taylors' Hall, Threadneedle Street, he
gave special thanks as a patriot and a practising Jew:

*Merchant Taylors Hall,
Threadneedle Street.*

*'. . . Believing that it is not a political office, and yet that it has duties both to the Queen
and to the public, I hope, in the execution of those duties, to swerve neither to the right nor
the left, but on the one hand to uphold the rightful prerogatives of the Crown, and on the
other to support the just liberties of the people. It is gratifying to find that, though
professing a different faith from the majority of my fellow-citizens, yet this has presented
no barrier to my desire of being useful to them in a situation to which my forefathers
would in vain have aspired; and I hail this as a proof that those prejudices are passing
away, and will pass away, which prevent our feelings from being as widely social, as
just, as comprehensive in their effect as the most amiable and best-instructed mind can
desire.'*

One of his first duties was to plan the procession for the Lord Mayor's Day
parade. He prepared it meticulously. Another duty, which he performed

superbly, was prison visiting. He began this immediately on 12 October 1837 with a visit to Newgate and to Whitecross Prisons. In the latter, he gave the governor £20 for distribution among deserving cases:

I found 428 unfortunate individuals confined within its walls. The men's wards were very unclean, but the women's extremely clean; there were only 24 females. The day rooms of the male prisoners were crowded with visitors. The prisoners were in good health, not more than 17 in the infirmary.'

In December he toured Newgate Prison, and the following March attended a Committee of Criminal Justice before visiting the prison to be present at the inquest on a prisoner who had died of typhoid fever. On 17 July 1838, he went to the Home Office to intercede on behalf of a prisoner named Rickie (a soldier who in a drunken stupor had shot an officer dead). Lord John Russell informed him that the sentence of capital punishment could not be commuted, but Sir Moses secured a reprieve. He found few who sympathised with him in his humane dislike of the death penalty, but there was no capital punishment when he was Sheriff. His dedication to this aspect of his office flourished. In one three-hour spell at Newgate he interviewed 142 prisoners; on another occasion he was at the Old Bailey in court when the sentences were pronounced: 'A most solemn and affecting scene. I went into the prison, and spoke with most of them afterwards.' At the Guildhall in September 1838 he reviewed this aspect of his office:

'Many of the duties of office myself and colleague have just passed through are of a painful nature. We have often been called upon to witness scenes of agony occasioned by want and crime. Some of this distress, however painful, we could not alleviate; but we have endeavoured to mitigate the sufferings of the prisoners, and to open to them better and happier courses of life, as far as public justice and the necessarily strict rules of a prison would permit.'

Five years later he was pleading the cause of two Poles (who had been in England only six weeks), imprisoned for hawking without a licence. He travelled to Chelmsford to see them in Springfield Gaol, and to gain their release. He drew up a petition for them and they were soon freed.

His diary for his year in office as Sheriff also mentions all the attendances at Court occasions, banquets, political meetings for the Jewish Emancipation Bill, and anniversary celebrations. His proudest moment came when he was

Lord John Russell.

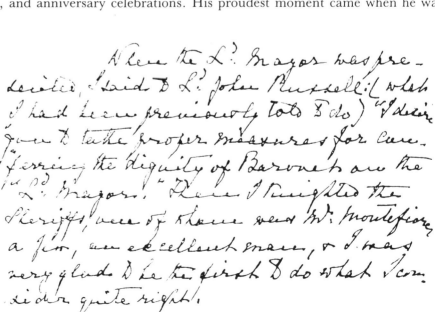

An extract from Queen Victoria's Journal for the 9th of November 1837.

knighted, 'Sir Moses', only the second Jew to be thus honoured. It was 9 November 1837:

'a day that can never be forgotten by me; it is a proud one: with the exception of the day I had the happiness of dedicating our Synagogue at Ramsgate, and the day of my wedding, the proudest day of my life. I trust the honour conferred by our most gracious Queen on myself and my dear Judith may prove the harbinger of future good to the Jews generally. On my kneeling to the Queen, she placed a sword on my left shoulder and said, "Rise, Sir Moses". I cannot express all I felt on this occasion. I had, besides, the pleasure of seeing my banner with "Jerusalem" floating proudly in the hall.'

During his year of office, Sir Moses, with his energy, popularity and compassion, made unprecedentedly large collections for the city's charities. The Mayor, Aldermen and Liverymen of the City of London, at the Guildhall, thanked him at the end of his year in office, for his dignity, hospitality, punctuality, zeal and judgement in performing his duties, support for charities, courtesy, and humanity to prisoners entrusted to his care. One of his successes was to get the sign 'Jews Walk' (on one of the walls of the Guildhall) taken down. The Lord Mayor ordered its removal. It was presented to Sir Moses and preserved by him in Judith, Lady Montefiore Theological College. He was also emphatic about Judaism during the Jews' Marriage Bill debate:

The sign marking the limit of 'Jews Walk' removed at Sir Moses' request and later presented to him.

'I am most firmly resolved not to give up the smallest part of our religious forms and privileges to obtain civil rights.'

The year had also been a time to celebrate the monarchy. Apart from his honours and visits to Buckingham Palace and the Queen's Drawing-Room, the Coronation festival preparations offered a brilliantly illuminated London. It was fitting that in August 1838, Sir Moses attended the meeting to consider a public monument to Lord Nelson, while the confidence of the age is epitomised in Sir Moses' Guildhall speech to toast Queen Victoria:

'that the reign of our now youthful Queen may be long and peaceful, and that her greatest glories may be connected with the universal education of her subjects, the diffusion of the most comprehensive principles of benevolence, charity, and love—principles which shall unite all in a desire to accomplish the proud wish that England may possess and exercise the great prerogative of teaching other nations how to live. Let our pride be in our civil advantages, in the security of our person and property, under a system of law and government which, whatever be its defects—and what is perfect on earth?—is at least as near to perfection as any government that has existed, or does now exist. Connected with the Corporation by high office, I feel a deep interest in its prosperity; and I pray that it may long exist to prove that popular corporate institutions are a bulwark to the throne, while they offer to the people a security for the preservation of their laws, and pure administration of justice.'

The Montefiores left England on 1 November 1838 for their second visit to Jerusalem and did not return until 5 September 1839. From 7 July 1840 to 26 February 1841 they were again abroad on the Mission to Mehemet Ali. On returning he presented to the Queen a copy of the decree obtained from the Sultan. She honoured him by granting supporters for his coat of arms 'being desirous of giving an especial mark of our Royal favour to the said Sir Moses Montefiore, in commemoration of these his unceasing exertions on behalf of his injured and persecuted brethren in the East, and the Jewish nation at large, have been graciously pleased to allow him to bear Supporters to his Arms, although the privilege of bearing Supporters be limited to the Peers of our Realm, the Knights of our Orders, and the Proxies of Princes of our Blood.' He averred that 'the supporters I wish for are to exalt our Holy religion by displaying "Jerusalem" in a more distinguished manner than I could have done'. In 1846 he received a Baronetcy from the Queen on the advice of Sir Robert Peel 'in consideration of your high character and eminent position in the ranks of a loyal and estimable class of Her Majesty's subjects agreeing with you in religious profession and in the hope that it may aid your truly benevolent efforts to improve the social conditions of the Jews in other countries by temperate appeals to the justice and humanity of their rulers'. Honoured and revered as a Jew and in recognition of his work in favour of Judaism, his position was unparalleled.

Sir Moses consistently upheld the authority of the Government of the day. As he recorded in his diary of 1848 on 10 April: 'It has been a day of much anxiety for the public peace, but, thank God! the Chartists' meeting has proved a complete failure.' Meanwhile, his endeavours centred upon the Board of Deputies, which had emerged as one of the main instruments as a Jewish organised pressure group. During these years, which included his opposition to the West London Reform movement, Sir Moses as President of the Board of Deputies, fought for pauper Jews excluded from outdoor relief, gained a clause placing synagogues on an equal footing regarding property and income as other places of worship, and won concessions for Jews in the Burials Bill and Factory Bill. He acknowledged the dichotomy between the honours given to him and the lack of formal political rights for Jews, for which he fought.

Sir Moses heading a delegation to Parliament demanding equal rights for Jews.

In February 1844 he and Board of Deputies' members approached the Prime Minister, Sir Robert Peel, regarding the removal of civil barriers, and at a state ball at Buckingham Palace in May, Peel told him that the campaign was prospering. In January 1845 Sir Moses judged that 'the time is now fitting for a recommencement of the agitation for Jewish emancipation'. A committee was elected, he and Baron Lionel de Rothschild discussed the issue with Sir Robert Peel at Downing Street, and a measure for enabling Jews to fill Corporation offices was shown to them. This was passed by both Houses in March, after a speech by the Duke of Cambridge complimenting the achievements of Salomons and Sir Moses as Sheriffs. (Sir Moses was made Sheriff of the County of Kent in February 1844, and Deputy Lieutenant of the County of Kent in 1847.)

The City of London elected Baron Lionel de Rothschild a Whig MP in 1847 but he could not sit in Parliament. The coalition of aristocrats, squires and Anglican bishops had successfully resisted Jewish participation in the Government, the final symbol of the triumph of the Whig middle class. A personal friend of Sir Moses, Prime Minister Lord John Russell introduced, in December 1847, a Bill for the removal of Jewish disabilities. It was carried by 256 to 186 votes. When the Bill was read a second time in February 1848, and passed by 277 votes to 204, Sir Robert Peel spoke for the cause of Jewish emancipation, with references to Sir Moses' humanitarian missions in Damascus and Russia:

> *'He carried with him letters of recommendation from British Ministers, certifying his high character for integrity and honour and the purity of the motives by which he was activated. How much more persuasive would those have been if they could have announced the fact that every ancient prejudice against the Jews had been extinguished here, and that the Jew was on a perfect equality as to civil rights, with his Christian fellow-citizen.'*

The Commons agreed, but the Lords defeated the Bill by 163 votes to 128, and Baron Lionel de Rothschild had to resign his seat. Sir Moses heard the debate in the Lords: 'It was a painful excitement. The majority against us was 35,

Sir Moses when given the freedom of the City of London on 6 October 1864.

much greater than was expected.' Eventually the Baron (Judith's sister's son) was permitted to take the oath on the Old Testament and became the first Jewish M.P. in 1858, Sir Moses as President of the Board of Deputies signing the following resolution:

> *'That this Board hails with the sincerest gratification the passing of the Bill affording to Her Majesty's subjects professing the Jewish religion the means of enjoying seats in the Legislature and that the grateful acknowledgements are especially due to the electors of the city of London, whose noble, untiring and enlightened labours have achieved a crowning victory in the cause of civil and religious liberty.'*

It was the vindication of a right, achieved by the liberals in the City of London and the respect which Jewish individuals had won among their fellow-citizens.

Sir Moses had been criticised in the early 1850s for not being sufficiently forceful in the search for full political emancipation. There had been controversy over this in the Board of Deputies, yet, in 1858, his gradualist philosophy had proved successful. It became his hallmark. His tactics were epitomised in his letter to Moroccan Jews in September 1864:

'Throughout the world, a chief characteristic of the Jews is that of being loyal, obedient, and peaceful subjects of their Sovereign. The precepts inculcating this conduct are enforced on us by the Sacred Scriptures, and by the wise exhortations of our Sages. Unless due respect be paid to the just exercise of legally constituted authority, there can be neither order nor safety though it may be that, in some places, the subordinate authorities abuse the powers with which they are entrusted, let it not be said that their severity or wrong-doing is attributable to any manifestation or disrespect on your part. You must never for a moment forget the loyalty, the affection and respect due to your Sovereign, on whom you must rely, and to whom, in case of need, you must appeal for protection against oppression, and redress for injury. It is by conduct such as this, we may hope that, under the Almighty's blessing, the hearts of those who would molest or injure you will be softened; or that, should injustice be done, it will be speedily and surely punished.'

The following month at the Guildhall he was given honorary freedom of the City of London for his sacrifices and journeys to alleviate the sufferings of Jews abroad and for his endeavours to alleviate the miseries of people of all creeds and denominations. Earl Shaftesbury approached Prime Minister, W. E. Gladstone, in 1868 on the possibility of raising Sir Moses to a peerage:

'The Jewish question has now been settled. The Jews can sit in both Houses of Parliament. There is a noble member of the house of Israel, Sir Moses Montefiore, a man dignified by patriotism, charity, and self-sacrifice, on whom Her Majesty might graciously bestow the honours of the Peerage. It would be a glorious day for the House of Lords when that grand old Hebrew were enrolled on the lists of the hereditary legislators of England.'

Gladstone.

Gladstone replied that the proposal would be carefully considered, but there the matter rested. The esteem felt for Sir Moses by Shaftesbury remained. When Sir Moses sent him a cheque of £15 for the poor children of the Ragged Schools in appreciation of Shaftesbury's benevolent activities, in July 1884, the latter wrote to the secretary of the Ragged School Union: 'That grand old Hebrew is better than many Christians.'

When Parliament authorised Oxford and Cambridge to award degrees to Jews in 1871 the last disability was removed. It was proof that justice could be obtained in this world, although western emancipation did not negate the possibility that a nationalist solution might be required to resolve the Jewish problem for the non-assimilated brethren in Eastern Europe and the Balkans; a rebirth of Jewish nationality which was internationalist in its support for all oppressed minorities. Sir Moses, when he resigned from his position as President of the Board of Deputies in August 1874, made intimations in this direction:

'I carry with me the unfading recollection of the sympathy and encouragement it has invariably afforded me at those important moments of my life, when, moved by the murmur of the oppressed or the cry of the afflicted, the Board deputed me to plead on its behalf, in distant lands, the cause of toleration and humanity . . . Long may our brethren in foreign countries receive from the Board a ready response when appealed to for aid or intercession.'

However, what coloured Sir Moses' convictions above all was loyalty to his Sovereign and scrupulous adherence to the laws of the nation. When the City of London presented an address to him for his 99th birthday, he expressed this:

'I rejoice in the reflection that any feeble efforts I may have made to advance the happiness and welfare of my fellow-creatures have been so kindly judged. With a fervent prayer for the health and long life of our gracious Queen, whose beneficent sway over this great and free country has caused so much happiness to all classes of her subjects . . .'

He also rejoiced in the Queen's telegrams congratulating him on his 'useful and honourable life' in 1883, and on 'a century of loyalty and philanthropy' in 1884, and a note 'trust you are well' in January 1885. Finally, on 10 July 1885 he rejoiced to hear that Lionel de Rothschild's son, Nathaniel, had taken his seat in the House of Lords. On 29 July, following Sir Moses' death, at a meeting of the Common Council, the Lord Mayor spoke of him as the most distinguished citizen of London and of his deep interests in the affairs of the citizens and their ancient Corporation.

The Royal Exchange 1821. Mr. Montefiore and Mr. N. M. Rothschild in the foreground. (The Trustees of the British Museum).

3. TRAVELS TO EGYPT AND THE HOLY LAND IN 1827

In the nineteenth century travelling abroad was precarious and fraught with complications. The first problem was the difficulty of acquiring a ship at a time when there were few passenger ships. Also to be negotiated were storms at sea, piracy, highwaymen, plagues, quarantines, battles and long delays in communication by mail. Because of the extraordinary dramas and escapes from drowning, Sir Moses' travels became a way of life between 1827 and 1875. He became renowned for visiting numerous countries to intercede for basic human rights of oppressed minorities and was not content to express his convictions from the comfort of his London home. Travel became the great passion of this extraordinarily energetic man, and his wife Judith accompanied him, and with fortitude and courage faced the perils of these voyages. After her death in 1862 he continued his journeys alone.

This first visit to Jerusalem in 1827 was a ten-month trip with only four days spent in the Holy City. Their departure had been a project planned since their marriage fifteen years earlier. In December 1825 Mrs. Montefiore had remarked in her diary of his 'mania for travelling' and exactly a year later Sir Moses wrote in *his* diary 'By the blessings of God, prepare for a trip to Jerusalem.' It was to be the most momentous step of his public life. He went to the Foreign Office and obtained letters of introduction from Lord Auckland for the Governor of Malta, to Admiral Codrington (commanding the Mediterranean Squadron) and to the British consuls in the Near East. This procedure was to give him a taste for foreign travelling under official or quasi-official auspices.

Lady Montefiore's handwritten Journal.

The travelling carriage used by the Montefiore's on their overseas travels.

On 1 May 1827 they set out from their home in London in their travelling carriage drawn by four horses. They took with them a portable bed and tents (in the absence of hotels) and a maid and a chef. They called first at the synagogue as was their custom before setting out on a perilous journey, Sir Moses being an extremely pious and observant Jew, meticulous in his fulfilment of religious injunctions.

Travel was an arduous process. It took them twelve hours to reach Dover, three months to reach Malta, and a further six weeks before they arrived in Jerusalem. At Dover their travelling carriage was put on board their ship and served as a cabin during the passage. Their route was by carriage to Naples, boat to Messina, by litter over the Sicilian mountains and from Capo Passero on a two-masted open row-boat for Malta. There they dined at the Palace, Sir

Above. *'Rise Sir Moses', the young Queen Victoria confers a knighthood on Sir Moses.*

Below left. *With the Egyptian Khedive Mehemet Ali Pasha.*

Below right. *In uniform as Lord Lieutenant of London.*

Moses delivering Lord Auckland's letter to the Governor, the Hon. F. C. Ponsonby. They visited the plantations of the silk company—5,000 mulberry trees were in this place. The Governor advised him to go to the East in a ship of war on account of Greek pirates, the state of lawlessness on the high seas, and the unstable state of Oriental politics. The Greek War made the overland route impossible.

In 1821 the Greeks has revolted against their Turkish overlords but the Sultan appealed to the pasha (governor) of Egypt, Mehemet Ali, who was nominally his vassal. The latter sent his son, Ibrahim, to subdue the islanders and made a landing in the Morea. By 1826 his savage policy of depopulation had almost annihilated the Greeks. Meanwhile, Britain's naval supremacy in the eastern Mediterranean to secure trading interests required that Russia be prevented from gaining control of the Straits of the Bosphorus and the Dardanelles. Prime Minister Canning had to act, and sent Wellington to St. Petersburg where a secret protocol was signed by which Russia and Britain agreed to intervene in Greece. The French government joined the agreement in the treaty of July 1827 signed in London, while the Montefiores were at sea on their way to Alexandria. In September French and British naval squadrons discovered the Turkish and Egyptian fleets in Navarino Bay.

The Leonidas.

Right. *The Pyramids and A View Near Cairo by Edward Lear (The Tate Gallery).*

Opposite in colour. *The Lord Mayor's Banquet in honour of Queen Victoria in her coronation year attended by Sir Moses at the Guildhall London, 16 November 1837.* (See pages 25 and 27 in text).

Moses had acquired Captain Anderson's the *Leonidas* to take them to Alexandria under convoy of the *Garnet* sloop of war at a cost of £550. This part of the journey took twelve days. They later celebrated Captain Anderson's birthday with an extra bottle of champagne, the travellers not having yet adopted the necessary abstemious habits of an Eastern climate.

They reached Alexandria on 27 August. Judith Montefiore kept a detailed diary of this journey and here are some of her impressions:

Monday, August 27. Alexandria.

'*At ten we quitted the Leonidas in Captain Anderson's boat, and for the first time set foot on the land where our nation had, as it were, its cradle; where our ancestors were persecuted, but grew up into a mighty people. The first view we had of this ancient city presented us with a scene of filth and desolateness. Many persons were swimming near the shore, and pigs and dogs were feeding on the refuse of the town along the banks. We passed through the narrow dirty streets, the novel sight of loaded camels and Turks on donkeys. We at once felt that we were no longer in Europe, or among Europeans.*'

Under the oppressive heat and incessant attacks by mosquitoes, they visited the relics of past grandeur. They were taken on a tour of the Pyramids by a Bedouin who had acted in the same capacity to Napoleon, and observed that in

Sir Moses with the Egyptian Khedive Mehemet Ali.

some of the narrow streets people slept at night on the ground with no other covering than a piece of mat or a cloak.

Sir Moses was presented by Mr. Salt, the British Consul General, to Mehemet Ali Pasha, and this interview laid the foundation of a lasting friendship. The Pasha was sufficiently impressed with his visitor that he asked him to act as his agent in England, but Moses' retirement from business made acceptance of this offer impracticable. However, when the Pasha's successor, Said Pasha, sent his son, Prince Toussoun, to England to be educated, his guardianship was confided to Sir Moses and Lady Montefiore. She commented on the Pasha:

Wednesday, September 5. Cairo.

'His extensive mercantile transactions were, however, a great source of jealousy and dissatisfaction to his subjects, who are thereby deprived of the advantages of competition and unfettered trade. He would not grant a farmer a longer lease than a year, and fixed the price of all the produce of the land himself. All his vast transactions are managed by himself, and every written document passes under his inspection. He told Montefiore that he never indulges in more than four hours' sleep during the night. He might prove a great character in the world were he entirely unfettered.'

For the Montefiores, the chances of going to Jerusalem from Alexandria seemed to be diminishing. There were delays in getting a ship owing to the plague in Acre, brigands, pirates, storms and incipient battles. They were informed that Abdallah, the Pasha of Damascus, was inimical to all Europeans and that they would run the risk of being murdered, or, as Mr. Salt warned, sold as slaves. Moses remarked laconically that travelling was 'not always divested of disagreeables', but later added:

'I think I more ardently desire to leave Egypt than ever our forefathers did. No one will ever recite the passover service (which gives an account of the exodus from Egypt) with more true devotion than I shall do, when it pleases Providence to restore me to my own country, and redeem me and my dear wife from this horrible land of misery and plague.'

Eventually, on 11 October, they succeeded in hiring Captain Jones of the *Henry William* to transport them to Jaffa, to wait while they visited Jerusalem and return them to Alexandria. On 16 October they arrived at Jaffa, Mrs.

Sir Moses with Lady Montefiore disguised in Turkish dress disembarking at Jaffa.

Montefiore attired in the Turkish bernische and white turban and veil in order to pass as a Moslem, but her husband refused to disguise himself. At first, the Governor would not allow British subjects to land, owing to the unsettled state of politics but the British Consul, Mr. Damiani, procured permission.

When they landed 'on that shore, where our ancestors suffered so severely from the treachery and invasion of other nations', the Ottoman Empire was a vast dynasty comprised of a mixture of races, languages and religions, held together only by subservience to an arbitrary central authority. It extended across the northern coast of Africa as far as Morocco and into the Balkans as far as the rivers Danube and Pruth. It had a firm base in Asiatic Turkey with territories extended from the Persian Gulf. Its ruling class was Turkish and Moslem, whereas many of the subject people were Christians and Jews. In Palestine itself, the arbitrary exercise of power by local rulers and antagonism to Western penetration into Palestine had kept the country insulated from the West. Napoleon had been here as well. When the Montefiores were received by the consul, they sat on the same divan in the same room once occupied by him.

The Agar, a stately Turk, was appointed to take the Montefiores to the Holy City. He exclaimed, 'I am come by order of my master, the Governor of Jaffa, to protect this respectable company to Jerusalem, during their continuance there, and on their way back; and this I will do with my hand.' As they rode to Ramlah on donkeys, they observed the roads lined with prickly pear, pomegranate, fig, orange and lemon trees, the finest they had ever seen, an experience which Moses utilised in his agricultural plans on subsequent visits to Jerusalem. From Ramlah, they rode to Jerusalem and at 5 p.m. on Wednesday 17 October they dismounted at their destination.

After an arduous journey lasting five and a half months they had arrived. Jerusalem revealed a picture of poverty and piety. Moslem reactions to the Greek War had created a vulnerable existence for the Christians and Jews in the city. In fact, the governor of the eyalet of Damascus (of which Jerusalem was a part) had sent a message to the Jerusalem Moslems forbidding them to

Riding towards Jerusalem.

35

kill non-Moslem subjects, but the Moslems had revolted against the governor in 1824.

Moses had travelled to Palestine in a spirit of pious pilgrimage but also with the practical aim of benefiting the Jewish inhabitants, 10,000 of whom lived in the four Holy Cities of Jerusalem, Safed, Tiberias and Hebron. The Governor expressed regret that he should stay in a Jewish home, but Moses, on hearing about the Governor's comment, retorted, 'I hope I shall ever live and die in the society of my brethren of Israel.' He visited the Wailing Wall and the Mosque of Omar, built on the site of Solomon's temple, and observed the olive, the fig-trees, and the vine covering many of Jerusalem's hills and roses flourishing in the valleys:

'No city in the world can have a finer situation than this, nor is there a better climate' he remarked in his diary. They also witnessed appalling scenes of desolation, as though the heart of the land had been broken. Judith expressed their sentiments:

Saturday, October 20. Jerusalem.

'Many were the solemn thoughts which rose in our minds, finding ourselves thus engaged in this holy land: the country of our ancestors, of our religion, and of our former greatness; but now, alas! of persecution and oppression. We hear from everyone of the extortions that are levied, and that there is no means of support except such as is provided by the bounty of other countries, with the exception of the little help afforded by the few families who continue here from a principle of religious enthusiasm, and contribute all in their power to the support of the necessitous.'

View of Jerusalem by Edward Lear (The Tate Gallery).

Rachel's Tomb before restoration by the Montefiores.

She visited Rachel's tomb:

Friday, October 19. Jerusalem.

'On entering I was deeply impressed with a feeling of awe and respect, standing as I thus did, in the sepulchre of a mother in Israel. The walls of the interior are covered with names and phrases chiefly in Hebrew and other Eastern characters; but some few English are to be found among them, and to these I added the names of Montefiore and myself. My feelings of gratitude on this occasion were not a little increased by a knowledge of the circumstance that only six European females are said to have visited Palestine in the course of a century.'

In a Greek convent, Judith observed that brass candlesticks had replaced the silver, which had been sacrificed to supply the exactions of the Turks, while very few Jewish families could support themselves.

Montefiore was one of the first Jews of distinction and wealth to visit Jerusalem in the early nineteenth century so the impact of his visit on this small oppressed Jewish community was immeasurable. The spiritual head of the Sephardi community, the Rev. Haham Moses Soozin, likened him to the coming of the Messiah, since he was wealthy enough to distribute gifts to the poor and sufficiently distinguished to be received and fêted by the Pasha and Jerusalem's notables. However, for Moses, the mere dispensing of charity had to be replaced by a policy to equip the indigent with the means of self-help.

He obtained some terra sancta from an ancient burial-ground to take home. He placed it under the Ark (the holiest part) of the Synagogue, built near the country home in Ramsgate, to commemorate this momentous visit to the Holy Land. After visiting a theological college, Etz-Khayim (Tree of Life), he went to see the Governor at the Palace, where he was offered coffee and pipes, and a eulogium was written on their passport to which the Governor affixed his name and seal. Moses offered a special prayer thanking the Almighty for permitting

*Jerusalem from the West.
(Bartlett)*

them to behold the Land of Promise. Judith exclaimed on the last day of this visit:

Sunday, October 21. Jerusalem.
'Farewell, Holy City! Blessed be the Almighty, who has protected us while contemplating the sacred scenes which environ thee. Thankful may we ever be for His manifold mercies!'

This brief stay in Jerusalem inflamed their love for the Holy Land, and the welfare of the inhabitants. The visit became a landmark in their life together. On his return, Moses replaced the Hebrew verses in the family blazon by one word 'Yerushalaim' written in Hebrew characters, and hung over his bed the words in Hebrew 'If I forget thee, O Jerusalem, may my right hand forget its cunning'. Henceforth, they devoted themselves to Eretz Yisrael and cemented their ardent commitment to Judaism and philanthropy. On Moses' birthday, 24 October, he wrote in his diary:

Sir Moses' bed inscribed in Hebrew 'If I forget thee, O Jerusalem, may my right hand forget its cunning.'

'This day I begin a new era. I fully intend to dedicate much more time to the welfare of the poor and to attend Synagogue as regularly as possible on Monday, Thursday and Saturday.'

By then, they were back on board the *Henry William*. Four days earlier, on 20 October, the battle of Navarino had been fought. Had it not been for the sluggishness with which news travelled, the departure from Turkish territory might have been even more precarious than it was. The Turkish and Egyptian fleets had been attacked and fifty of Ibrahim's ships sunk, Admiral Codrington (who favoured the Greek cause) having received ambivalent instructions which allowed him to use force 'if necessary'. When the Montefiores returned to Alexandria, Arab women were lamenting the disaster in the streets. The

Montefiores' return journey by sea tempted providence. Vessels preceding them had been attacked by Greek buccaneers, and the *Henry William* was 'greeted' by four large guard-boats, Turkish men-of-war full of soldiers, who mistook them for Greeks:

Friday, October 26. The Henry William.

'On seeing us, they approached, calling out in Arabic, to know what we were, whence we came, and to what nation we belonged. Our pilot and dragoman could not satisfy them till they came near enough to have ocular as well as oral demonstration, that we were really and truly Inglese. A cannon mounted on each boat, the pistols, guns, and cutlasses with which the men were armed, together with their red, Turkish uniform, presented a formidable spectacle.'

Having reassured the Turks, they were waiting to be guided into the harbour of Alexandria when a huge explosion occurred:

'The effect continued for some time, forming a body in the air like an enormous tree. We found that the explosion was from a ship. It was a Turkish frigate, the commander of which, it was stated, having had some difference with the Pasha, and fearing that he should be put in chains, had set a lighted match to the magazine, and blown up the ship.

Alexandria, showing the original site of 'Cleopatra's Needle'. (Richard Lepsius 1853)

Seven or eight midshipmen were destroyed with the frigate. The event created little excitement at Alexandria, where such instances of human sacrifice were not uncommon.'

After landing safely, Moses was informed that the Pasha expected a war of religion which would last for fifty years and had issued a proclamation calling for all true Moslems to protect their religion and begin fortifications. Six vessels had entered the harbour, every one of which had been plundered by pirates. Moses mused:

'I have every reason to believe that for the last three months we are the only persons, sailing without a convoy, who have escaped.'

News reached Alexandria of the battle of Navarino on 2 November and spread consternation among European residents, although the Pasha pledged their protection in his territories. He did not seem unduly perturbed by the loss of his fleet since he had already ordered more to be built in Marseilles, Leghorn and Trieste.

On 7 November, the Montefiores left Egypt on the *Leonidas*, sailing under the protection of the French schooner, *La Dauphinoise*, in a convoy consisting of four French, three British, one Austrian and one Russian vessel. Mrs.

Montefiore's parting words in her diary express their thoughts:

Wednesday, November 7. The Leonidas.

'the state of politics, which rendered our situation insecure, the detentions, the contrarities, and obstacles we had experienced in getting away, made us quit this once celebrated city with, perhaps, as much satisfaction as we felt on arriving in it. The captain announced that a squall was approaching, and we hastened down to the cabin, to avoid, if possible, the threatened evil.'

Nineteen days later, and still at sea, Moses recorded a significant event. Subsequently, on the first night of the Passover Festival, he used to read this extract from his diary of Monday evening, 26 November 1827:

'Since Friday last we had encountered continual gales of wind with a heavy sea. This morning the sky again assumed its most threatening aspect, dark clouds arising in all directions, Captain Anderson foretelling a repetition of the late dreadful weather. At this awful pause, a little before noon, I threw into the sea a small piece of my last year's Passover cake laid by on the evening of the Agada, supplicating the Almighty to protect us and to avert the coming tempest, likewise to tranquillize the still-troubled Ocean. Between 7 and 8 o'clock in the evening. It is with the warmest gratitude I humbly acknowledge the Almighty's kind interposition on our behalf. The clouds which appeared to everyone on board so dreadfully threatening during the morning, have as it were by a miracle, dispersed, and instead of pouring their fury upon us the sea also became every hour more and more tranquil.'

However, four days' later, when only a mile from the port at Malta, (everyone expecting to anchor within the hour), another unforgettable experience happened. Moses penned it vividly:

'How frail are human joys; most suddenly the wind had changed again to the west, and commenced blowing in a terrific manner. Thus, in an instant, were our hopes gone, and we were blown off the land, a tremendous sea obliging us to take to our beds. God only knows when we shall reach Malta.'

Saturday December 1:

'The last was a dreadful night; it blew almost a hurricane: a frightful sea: the ship rolled and pitched so as to occasion serious alarm to all on board. Poor Judith suffered severely. The captain had never in his life experienced a worse night. I shall never forget the night, but on each Sabbath eve shall recollect with gratitude God's mercy in saving us from destruction.'

The following day they landed at Malta, having spent more than three months in Captain Anderson's company and slept sixty-eight nights on board his ship. Moses was to be the emissary from the battle zone, because the Governor requested to be informed how the news of the battle of Navarino had been received at Alexandria. Moses wrote him an account of it. He also had a visit from Captain Lewis Davies, of the *Rose*, who described the battle of Navarino from the view-point of a participant, while a ship arrived from Constantinople bearing the news that the ambassadors had left and all allied ships were put under embargo.

On 22 December Moses visited Admiral Codrington who had been fascinated by his description of the Pasha's reception of the Navarino news. Codrington clarified his reasons for commencing hostilities, claiming that since the Turks had not listened to his speaking-trumpet he had to use cannon; he would have attacked earlier but for adverse winds and the position of the French fleet. He entrusted Montefiore with despatches on the battle to Lord Burghersh at Florence and the Duke of Clarence (later William IV).

In subsequent visits, one of the motives behind Moses' involvement in Palestine became his desire to encourage British interests generally in the area.

Galloping horses speed Sir Moses' carriage with despatches of the battle of Navarino.

But, in 1827, his close association with British officialdom in an age of expanding British power (as shown in these contacts in Malta) prompts the query whether the Foreign Office was planning to use him as an instrument of British foreign policy. This association was illustrated on his return to England in his audience with His Royal Highness who asked Moses what people in the East were saying of Navarino. He answered 'that it could not be prevented, for, as the British commander himself said, "when the British flag is insulted, an English admiral knows what is his duty!" '

The Montefiores left Malta on 2 January on Captain Copeland's H.M.S. *Mastiff* for Naples. Moses delivered Codrington's letter for Lord Burghersh in Florence and reached Leghorn on 1 February. They hurried back in their carriage to Calais, but even so did not arrive in Dover until 28 February.

In England the news of Navarino had been heard with mixed feelings among Government circles. Destruction of the Turkish fleet seemed to offer the Russian Government carte blanche to extend their Empire. Moses went to London and the Admiralty to deliver Codrington's letters and the next day to the Duke of Clarence. Although he now placed himself under the care of a physician, in order to recover from the rigours of ten months' travelling, what engaged Moses was his project for future educational facilities in the Holy Land.

Within two years, the British Government had reverted to its old policy in the Near East, supporting Turkey against Russia. When the Montefiores next visited Jerusalem in 1839 the structure of the Ottoman Empire had been further loosened by the French conquest of Algeria, recognition of Serbia, Moldavia and Wallachia as autonomous principalities, and the emergence of Egypt as another autonomous region. The British Government buttressed Turkey against Russia but condemned the corrupt and brutal methods by which the Turks misgoverned their Christian and Jewish subjects. Sir Moses' work in Palestine was about to begin in earnest.

4. MISSION TO MEHEMET ALI, KHEDIVE OF EGYPT

with extracts from Sir Moses' Diary, 1840

One of the great unsolved mysteries of the last 150 years was the disappearance in Damascus on 5 February 1840 of Father Thomas (a Franciscan friar) and his servant Ibrahim Amara. The friar had lived in Damascus for 33 years as a doctor vaccinating people against smallpox. Suddenly numerous prominent Jews were accused of ritual murder. This absurd and baseless slander was that Jews killed Christians in order to mix their blood in the preparation of matzot, the unleavened bread eaten during Passover in remembrance of the Exodus from Egypt. The blood libel had been in circulation in the East as early as the fifteenth century, although the early Christians had been accused of using human blood for their ceremonies before they had turned the accusation against Jews. The result in 1840 was a savage wave of arrests, excruciating tortures to enforce confessions, plunder of Jewish homes and open incitement to hatred of all Jews in Damascus.

Damascus.

Lord Palmerston (National Portrait Gallery).

On 15 June 1840, at a meeting of the Board of Deputies, Sir Moses was requested to proceed with Crémieux and Munk to Alexandria and Damascus. Lord Palmerston wrote privately to Sir Moses:

'Despatches will be prepared to be conveyed by you to the several British Agents in the East, acquainting them with the objects of your journey, recommending you to their protection and enjoining them to use their influence with the authorities in their respective districts, to obtain for you every facility for the prosecution of your enquiries and to secure you as far as possible from injury and molestation during your stay in the East.'

Anglo-Jewry in the person of Sir Moses could sail on the rising tide of British power and prestige, while Palmerston used the righting of Jewish inequalities as a cause for British intervention, just as the French intervened to protect Catholics. In his diary of 1840, Sir Moses recorded, on the evening of 6 July:

I was employed writing letters and making up accounts, although extremely fatigued. My dear Jud went to bed at midnight. I remained up. May the Almighty God of our Fathers, Abraham, Isaac and Jacob, bless with complete success our Mission and bring us in peace and safety back to our friends.'

The next day, Sir Moses left London accompanied by his wife, Crémieux, Munk and Dr. Loewe, and including Mr. Wire (his former under-sheriff, later Lord Mayor of London) and Dr. Madden, his personal physician.

Setting sail.

Dr. L. Leowe.

Dr. Loewe was a brilliant linguist with a knowledge of thirty-nine languages. He had first met the Montefiores in 1835 and was subsequently invited to stay with them at Ramsgate. He was requested by Sir Moses to draw up a plan for travels in Palestine. While in Rome in 1839 Loewe met Sir Moses by chance, and decided to become his secretary and interpreter of Oriental languages. They became life-long companions on twelve philanthropic missions abroad. Dr. Loewe assisted Sir Moses with much of his foreign correspondence and was consulted on numerous public and personal matters. They shared a pragmatic approach to integration as the route to Anglo-Jewish emancipation and a similar conservative respect for rabbinic institutions. Dr. Loewe became Sir Moses' closest confidante and aide. Together they promoted the growth of the yishuv in Palestine and sought to secure Jewish civil rights everywhere in every country they visited. As the first principal of the Judith, Lady Montefiore College in 1869 he was given Judith's journals and diaries to assist in a memoir. Instead, as Dr. Loewe wrote in 1887,

'I found it impossible to write a Memoir of Lady Montefiore without making it at the same time, a Memoir of Sir Moses himself, both of them having been so closely united in all their benevolent works and projects.'

He was able to consult eighty-five diaries which Sir Moses had written between 1814 and 1883, and completed the *Diaries of Sir Moses and Lady Montefiore* six months before his own death.

Dr. Loewe began his own diary on 7 July:

'Sir Moses engaged me for the Mission to act in the quality of Secretary and Interpreter of Oriental and Modern languages.'

and Sir Moses began his Diary of the Mission:

'we proceeded to the London Bridge Wharf where we were met by the German and Portuguese Congregations, and very many others of our brethren; Mr. Aaron Joseph, Sam Cohen, J. Hillier's father and brother. I should think there were more than a hundred Jews waiting to see us set off, all giving us their blessing, wishing us health, success and safe return. They came on board the boat with us and shook hands with me on taking leave of us. This mark of kindness on the part of so many of our brethren was most cheering to us. The carriages were on board boat. Evening. I was much fatigued with writing and want of my natural rest, and my feelings were much excited by the scene I witnessed on the wharf and on board the boat, so great the number of kind and good people leaving their beds at unseasonable hour to offer us their good wishes and blessings, well knowing how undeserving I am of such honour. I can only pray to the God of my Fathers to crown my Mission with success for the glory of His holy name and for the peace of His children the people of His choice and of His Covenant. It was blowing very hard when we reached Gravesend, we determined to land, which was not effected without some difficulty and inconvenience. Both Jud and Mr. Wire got very wet.'

The next day, the travellers boarded the *Arrow*:

'Laus Deo. Wednesday 8th of July. Dover. The Ship Hotel. Calais. Hotel Quillacq. About half past eight the mail and several passengers were brought on board and we started. Blowing hard with a heavy sea, and reached the French coast before 11 o'clock. Boats came alongside, the bags and some 5 passengers were with some difficulty put into them. The weather being squally and a heavy sea we and many others would not venture, the Captain deeming it more prudent for us to remain on board till the vessel could enter. We came to anchor and remained rolling about till after four o'clock, my poor Judith dreadfully sick. Dr. Loewe not much better, Mr. Wire and myself tolerably well.'

Having reached France, they travelled in their carriage to Paris and met members of the Rothschild family there, and later in Naples. Sir Moses was to be advised by Baron Charles in Naples on the subject of the Mission:

'He commended the most conciliatory means to speak with the French Consul and indeed with everyone that might be useful to us, appealing to their humanity and to assure them that it mainly depended on them my success. Baron Charles said his father had often taught him when he had occasion to apply to an inferior or to a man who had little power to assist him in carrying his object he had in view, he spoke with the person as though the whole depended entirely on him, though perhaps he knew he had but the smallest possible influence on the business. Baron Charles said he would go to Rome and endeavour to obtain from the Pope an introduction for Dr. Madden, he being a Catholic, to the Church authorities in Damascus in Syria.'

That journey to Naples was eventful. Sir Moses' account of each day's experiences is a unique record:

Laus Deo. Thursday 16th July. Chalons. Lyons.

We left Chalons at 6, breakfasted at Macon, reached Lyons Hotel de l'Europe ½ past 6. Weather has been oppressively hot, temperature 81. I am dreadfully fatigued but must be off tomorrow before 4.

Laus Deo. Friday 17th July. Lyons.

We were all up at 3. Most of our party were complaining. Dr. Madden had been frightened out of his bed by rats and taken refuge on the Sopha in the sitting-room. All agree the Hotel de l'Europe a most extravagant and dirty house. Rode to the Rhine and embarked on board the L'Aigle. The heat has been great all day, thermometer 88 in the carriage at half past 3. My handsome travelling cap flew overboard and was lost. Thanks to Almighty God we reached Avignon in safety at 5.20. Walked to the Hotel du Palais Royal, we dressed, read our prayers, were much vexed to find our dinner was not kosher, though Monsieur Crémieux wrote to say our host was a Jew and we should have everything we wanted.

Laus Deo. Saturday 18th July. Avignon. Hotel du Palais Royal.

My dear Jud, Dr. Loewe and I went to the Synagogue this morning at ½ past 7. The Synagogue is going rapidly to decay. About 40 Jewish families, not strict and little devotion. I was very weak, and layed nearly the whole day on the Sopha. Precisely at 10 Monsieur Crémieux arrived from Nimes. We left Avignon ½ past 10. Dr. Madden and Dr. Loewe outside on carriage. Mr. Wire, Monsieur Crémieux in the open one. My stomach dreadfully out of order all night. I was in much pain, we felt the heat of the travelling terribly oppressive. Our host and hostess were extremely civil.

Laus Deo. Sunday 19th July. Marseille, Hotel Beau.

We reached this place at ½ past 9 dreadfully fatigued and very weak, our bowels being out of order. We breakfasted, several persons paid us visit, Mons. and Madame Crémieux, Mr. Cohen and his father the Grand Rabbin. We went on board the Minos *to see our cabins, those reserved for me and J very bad, Mme Crémieux having secured very good ones for herself and party. We are at a great loss for a lady's maid.*

Laus Deo. Monday 20th July. Marseille.

Mr. Turnbull, the British Counsul, called on me. I called on Messrs. Roux de Fraissenel and company, presented my letter and drew £300.'

Laus Deo. Tuesday 21st July. Marseille. At Sea.

'Soon after 6 this morning I and my dear Jud and Dr. Loewe rode to the Synagogue and prayed to the God of our Fathers, the Almighty Maker of Heaven and Earth, for the safety and success of our Mission. We dined at 3, having sent the luggage and servants on board. The evening blew very fresh when we first started but the evening was fine. Mr. Moore, Queen's Messenger, and Mr. Doyle of the Chronicle *are fellow passengers.*

Laus Deo. Wednesday 22nd July. At Sea.

The night was fine and the sea smooth, the wind north-east. I am most grateful for a good night's rest. Weather dreadfully hot. We dined on our kosher meat. I remained on deck till after midnight.

Laus Deo. Thursday 23rd July. Leghorn.

The Blessed God of our Fathers, Abraham, Isaac and Jacob in His great Mercy and Goodness brought us in safety and peace again to my native city. The boat came to an anchor at 7. As usual we went to the Hotel Globe. We had many visitors as soon as we were on shore. A deputation from the Synagogue. I requested they would be so kind as to have Minha said soon after 12, at which hour I went there. We said Minha and afterwards the Haham said a prayer for success of our Mission. We immediately after prayers returned to our ship. Weather beautifully fine but very hot before leaving Leghorn. I wrote to our dear and honoured mother, also to Lionel de Rothschild, enclosing one to the Committee. The night was calm and starlight, we passed very close to the Isle of Elba. I retired early being much fatigued, the ankles greatly swollen.'

Sir Moses was as anxious about the outcome of the Mission as relatives in London. He voiced his doubts to Louis Cohen in a letter:

'Do not believe that the affairs of Damascus can be settled as speedily as we had hoped, indeed I fear it is only part of a deep plot against the Jews, not only in the East, but in Europe. Heaven grant I may be mistaken.'

'Laus Deo. Friday 24th July. Civita Vecchia.

At Leghorn it was recommended to me not to land here, as there has been some little movement against the Israelites occasioned by the writings of a priest called Meyer, a converted Jew. Louis Cohen's apprehensions are not without foundations. At Leghorn just before Passover a woman lost a child and accused the Jews of stealing it, but the Governor put her into prison and said she should remain there till the child was found. This had the desired effect, the child was found the next day, the incident was kept as quiet as possible, the Jews begged of me not to mention it. We left Civita Vecchia 3.10. Extremely hot, not a breath of air. I went into my berth and prepared for Sabbath, washed, I have read my prayers.

Laus Deo. Saturday 25th July. Naples.

Last night was beautifully starlight, smooth sea, the thermometer 81 in our cabin. This morning read our prayers and then we came to an anchor in the harbour of Naples. A few minutes afterwards the two eldest sons of Baron Charles de Rothschild came on board to invite us to his house. It being Sabbath we could not avail ourselves of his kindness. Mons. and Madame Crémieux went with the Captain to Pompeii. Baron Charles sent us presents of two fine large turkeys, a dozen of old Hock and a box of sweetmeats. He came himself at 3 o'clock with his eldest son. I had a long conversation with him on the subject of my Mission. He sent me afterwards a letter of introduction to Mr. Laurin of Alexandria.

Laus Deo. Sunday 26th July 1840.

I did not leave the deck till near one this morning. We passed a most disagreeable night, the vessel rolled so much though no wind.

Laus Deo. Monday 27th July. At Sea.

I did not leave the deck till after 12 last night. The air was cooler, the sea smooth, and we rested well. I rose at 6. We were still near the coast of Sicily. We have on board Mr. Moore, Queen's Messenger, and Mr. Lancaster, the gentleman who prepared the plan for the new church at Malta. He is returning from a mission to Queen Caroline, who has promised to visit Malta next April with the Bishop of London to be present at its dedication. The Jews appear under the greatest alarm in Italy, at Leghorn, I should believe, without much reason; at Rome I fear they have great cause. Mr. Scala said both the Pope and his Government were extremely against the Jews and had expressed a belief of the murder of Father Tomassio. The Pope had refused to confirm two Bulls issued by former Pontiffs when similar charges were brought against the Jews. The Christians seemed to believe if the Jews were innocent, then the Christians must be guilty of conspiracy against them, so God help us! ¼ to 2 Malta has been seen, a great breeze carrying us rapidly through the waters. We entered the harbour of Malta, Blessed by the Almighty God of Israel, in safety at 5 o'clock. We soon landed, went to Dunsford's Hotel, I paid my respects to the Governor at the Palace.

Laus Deo. 28th July. Malta.

My dear Jud and I rose at 5. Dr. L went with us at 6 to the Synagogue where we said our prayers. We left our cards afterwards at the Palace. I drew £260 at 30 days' sight on N. M. Rothschilds and Son on account of the Damascus Fund. My dear Jud and I with Dr. Loewe and Mr. Wire went on board the Eurotas. *May the Almighty God of our Fathers, God of Israel, conduct us in peace and comfort to the desired port of our voyage without the inconvenience of too much sea! The weather is fair but it is blowing very hard, N.N.W. We left the harbour of Malta at 1 o'clock. We found a very rough sea outside, which was terribly disagreeable. Those who have the happiness of remaining at home can have no idea of the misery of the sea, but I confide in the God of Israel for protection and consolation. I trust the sea will subside as the sun goes down. My dear Jud is very unwell, I am not much better.*

Laus Deo. 29th July. At Sea.

I was lying on deck until after 12 when Dr. Madden came and persuaded me to go to my cabin, and assisted me below. My dear Jud was on the floor of the Captain's cabin on the deck. The same weather continues today, blowing very fresh, N. wind, and a most disagreeable rolling sea. Wind favourable but fresh. There is a most annoying smell on board this boat, bilge water or bad oil coming from the engine. At ½ past 6 we had some heavy squalls of rain, my dear Jud was on the deck sitting on a stool, a lurch of the vessel threw her down backwards with great force. Both she and I were much alarmed but thanks to Heaven she was but little hurt, though frightened. The weather continued very rough, a most rolling sea. I remained all night in my clothes in one of the little cabins near the wheels of the engine on deck. There is the smell of the bilge water unbearable below. My dear Jud in the Captain's cabin, much lightning.

Laus Deo. Thursday 30th July. At sea.

The night was very rough with a terrible rolling sea, and this morning the weather was no better. I fear we are making little way as the vessel rolled so much. Oh may I never forget my total helplessness at this moment, but to the God of my Father, the Great God of Israel, I rely for help to calm the troubled ocean. Oh the misery of a sailor's life no tongue can express. About 1 o'clock we first got sign of land, Cape Horon in the Morea. The sea became less agitated, and most grateful I am for it. Mons. Crémieux has suffered much from sea-sickness. We passed Cape Matapan, then the Island of Serigo and entered the Greek Archipelago. Thanks to the Almighty the night was fine and calm and starlight.

Laus Deo. Friday 31st July, 1840. At sea.

Last night I had my old quarters in the little cabin on deck. Without taking off my clothes, I slept pretty well and rose at 5. Being Rosh Hadest said the Halel, etc. It is now ½ past 7. A lovely morning, smooth sea, light breeze. We are close in, with Falkner's Island north of us and the Island of Milo at the E.S.E. How different are our feelings this morning to those of yesterday. ½ past 9. Lovely mid deep blue sea, soon after 11 the heat of the sun compelled me to take refuge in the cabin, where I wrote a few lines to my dear Mother to be sent from Syra. ¼ before 5 we had the happiness to cast anchor in the bay, pretty close to Syra. The water is here extremely blue, but so clear that we could see the bottom 60 feet deep. We had prepared everything for going immediately on board the vessel that was to take us to Alexandria, but we learnt with regret that she had not yet arrived from Athens. We were consequently compelled to remain on board the Eurotas. *I shaved and prepared for Sabbath. My dear Judith, I and Dr. L read our prayers together after dinner. Most of the passengers went on shore to see the town. At night the town had a fairy-like appearance, thousands of lights, sparkling to the summit of the hill.'*

They were about to board their sixth vessel on this voyage:

'Laus Deo. Saturday, August 1st, 1840. Syra.

A lovely morning but very hot. We read our prayers and at ½ past 12 we left the Eurotas *and went on board the* Tancred. *We had most interesting prospects of the several islands in the Morea, particularly of the Island of Neros. The sunset was the most splendid I had ever seen. We had our Psalms with Dr. Loewe and Evening Prayers. A boat with soldiers remained close to the steamer till we left Syra. The night was beautifully clear, young moon and stars. I slept in my dear Jud's cabin, took a blue pill on retiring by Dr. Madden's advice.*

Laus Deo. Sunday 2nd August. At sea.

A magnificent day, cool air, brave breeze, 10 knots an hour, lively sea. Dear Jud is active and studious as ever.

Laus Deo. Monday 3rd August, 1840.

The weather is fine this morning, a fair wind but a rolling sea, which impedes our way, otherwise we might have reached Alexandria this evening. I rose soon after 5 o'clock. We have a lovely day, lively dancing sea, which gave us good spirits. At 12 o'clock we were 45 miles distant from Alexandria; the wind blowing very fresh. The sea rose considerably, we had the considerable expectation of reaching Alexandria before sunset, but we lost that hope at 6, not having yet sight at hand.

Laus Deo. Tuesday 4th August. At Sea.

I rose at 5 after passing a very uneasy night. 7 at Alexandria, but blowing and rolling terribly. We dropped anchor in the harbour of Alexandria ¼ to 8. The harbour is filled with men-of-war, Turkish and Egyptian.'

Sir Moses immediately visited the leader of the Jewish community, to ascertain the latest news from Damascus. The history of the affair was complex but can be briefly clarified.

A Moslem holy city, Damascus was the capital of Syria, which had in 1832 been invaded by the army of Mehemet Ali under the command of Ibrahim Pasha. The city was divided into Moslem, Christian and Jewish sections. Much of the trade and industry was run by Christians and Jews although sectarian rivalries and economic jealousies were increasing. The courts administered Islamic law but were corrupt; bribery often served as fees, false witnesses could be hired, torture was regularly employed to extort confessions. The official show trial for the death of Father Thomas and his servant had begun on 15 February, and by the end of April, 4 Jews had died from their tortures, 129 Jews were in prison, 65 boys from a religious school had been put in a dungeon (to persuade their parents to 'confess'), most of the local Jewish population had fled from the town, and 10 condemned men awaited death.

This outrageous situation had been promoted by the political uncertainties of Mehemet Ali's rule in Syria. With Ibrahim and the local Governor Sherif, he was dependent on French help to maintain conquests in the Turkish Empire and defy the European allies of the Sultan. The French consul in Damascus, Ratti-Menton, had reported the disappearance of Father Thomas to Sherif Pasha, had arrested and interrogated the suspects, and mounted the show trial with unscrupulous violence. It was he who had accused the local Jewish community of having abducted Father Thomas and of planning to use the body for ritual murder purposes; in the mock judicial enquiry he used his own spies as witnesses and formally demanded of the Governor the execution of the prisoners. (His rôle in the Damascus Affair remains a sensitive issue today. In the Father Thomas dossier in the archives of the French Quai d'Orsay in Paris, three despatches from Ratti-Menton have vanished from the file.)

The scandal had taken on international significance with the accusation of

Isaac Piciotto for complicity in the murder of the servant. Piciotto was an Austrian-protected person. Merlato, the Austrian consul, refused to give up his custody to Ratti-Menton and reaffirmed Austrian jurisdiction over Piciotto. 'The Damascus Affair' had been instantly circulated through the chancellories of Europe, with the simultaneous accusation of the ritual murder of a boy on the island of Rhodes on 21 February. Riots against Jews had occurred in several Syrian towns and at Djabor near Damascus the synagogue was sacked. It seemed as if the whole of Eastern Judaism was about to be engulfed in a wave of fanaticism.

News of the Damascus trials and the Rhodes incident had reached London on 27 March in a letter from the Constantinople Elders to Messrs. de Rothschild. When approached by the Rothschilds, French Minister, Thiers, and Pope Pius IX had refused to intervene, although Metternich sent a letter calling for clemency to Mehemet Ali. The Elders' letter had been submitted to the Board of Deputies at a meeting in Sir Moses' home on 21 April. This meeting condemned 'those false and atrocious charges, so frequently brought against the Jews during the middle ages' and asked French, British and Austrian Governments to remonstrate. For British Jews, the new blood libel was a source of the deepest anxiety. Revival of so sinister an appeal to vulgar fears and prejudices during the critical struggle for their political emancipation was potentially disastrous. They had requested a conference with Secretary of State for Foreign Affairs, Lord Palmerston.

On 30 April, a Board of Deputies' Committee had met Palmerston who promised to use his influence with Mehemet Ali and the Turkish Government to stop the atrocities. The British Foreign Office was also determined to undermine the hegemony of Ali and France in the Near East, and Ali had been sufficiently pressured to arrange for a judicial commission of European consuls to investigate the charges against the Jews. Thiers opposed it, so the proposal was dropped. A collection to defray the expenses of the mission to Damascus had brought in £6,674, Sir Moses contributing a third (£2,200). He was now the accredited representative of British Jews, supported by Peel, Palmerston, the British Government, and public opinion. (Crémieux, a Radical French politician, was to become Minister of Justice in 1848 and President of the international Alliance Israélite Universelle in 1863; Solomon Munk was later appointed secretary of the Central Consistory of the Jews in France.)

In the House of Commons, on 19 June, Sir Robert Peel had denounced the tortures inflicted upon the prisoners and alluded to the connivance of some Christian authorities, which 'reflected disgrace and dishonour on the age in which we live'. Three days later, Palmerston announced in the House that he had served notice on Mehemet Ali concerning the impression which the barbaric treatment aroused in Europe, and on 24 June Sir Moses with Baron Lionel de Rothschild went to the Foreign Office where Palmerston read to them despatches to Colonel Hodges and Lord Ponsonby at Constantinople. These urged the Pasha to compensate the sufferers and remove officials who had misconducted themselves in Damascus.

Sir Moses had introductions to the British representatives and could use his intermediaries with local rulers, but he was primarily the spokesman for British Jews. The Damascus Affair had been like an earthquake that shook Jewry to its foundation. He was to make it a turning-point in the chequered fortunes of his people. His active and dominant influence in the course of Jewish international events had begun, and the sympathy of the British Government, Foreign Secretary and Ambassadors was crucial in this first significant intervention by him overseas. At a crowded meeting in the Egyptian Hall in the Mansion House, the Lord Mayor of London expressed sympathy for the plight of the prisoners and wishes for the success of the mission. Sir Moses had also attended the Queen's drawing room.

Apart from apprehension as to the prisoners' safety, the heat in Alexandria was stifling, Lady Montefiore and Dr. Loewe were ill, and the political situation was very tense. The Four Powers (Britain, Prussia, Austria and Russia) were angling for a settlement to prevent Mehemet Ali consolidating his control over Syria; Ali was sympathetic to the French consul, Cochelet, on the delicate issue of the Damascus Affair. This was confirmed by Colonel Hodges, the British Consul General in Alexandria.

'At 10 I walked to Colonel Hodges', said he wished to go over the whole business with me, it had assumed a political character. I should find Mr. Cochelet, the French Consul, very plausible and very firm.'

On 5 August Hodges accompanied Sir Moses to the Palace:

'I rode with Colonel Hodges and read to him the petition I had to present to His Highness the Pasha of Egypt. He said he approved of it and hoped it would be granted, but did not by his manner appear to believe that it would. On our arrival we were immediately ushered into the Hall of Audience.'

Mehemet Ali was seated where Sir Moses had last talked to him on 13 July 1839. Dressed in uniform, Sir Moses was courteously received and presented his petition. This clarified that Judaism abhorred the use of blood in any form, that he had come to discover the truth in the Affair and to request the Viceroy to grant the authority for him to go to Damascus and to acquire a firman (decree) from him. He was disappointed:

'Nothing could have been less satisfactory than the interview, very different from my two former ones, he did not speak a single word to me; in my former interviews he was most friendly and chatty. I find Mons. Cochelet was with him last Wednesday for an hour and a half. The God of Israel help and protect us poor Jews. We are not likely to have any other. I was most out of spirits all day.'

However, Sir Moses records the volte-face:

'Laus Deo. Thursday 6th August. Alexandria.

I determined on going to the Pasha. It was near 9 when we entered the Palace. His

Sir Moses with the Egyptian Khedive Mehemet Ali 1840.

Mehemet Ali.

reception was most affable and kind, very different to that of yesterday. He was going away. He would be back on Friday and would give me an answer.
Laus Deo. Friday 7th August. Alexandria.
Mons Laurin sent a message that the Pasha had told him he would grant our request. I wrote to London.'

Yet the Pasha had other matters on his mind; difficulty suppressing a revolt in Northern Syria and a British fleet under Commodore Napier intercepting his warships! A Turkish steamer brought the Ultimatum of the Four Powers to Ali at the same time Louis Philippe was offering him men, money and ships.

The Mission was in jeopardy. Sir Moses was frustrated, having been counselled by Colonel Hodges not to venture to Damascus. The Pasha refused the Ultimatum. Sir Moses wrote to Louis Cohen:

'France is exerted in every way against us; it poisons the minds of the people against all Jews and most persons in this city. Should the late horrid conspiracy be hushed up by the liberation of the four important men in Damascus, I have no doubt other or similar charges would be brought against the Jews in a short time both in the East and in Europe.'

He was disappointed with the British Consul, Mr. Werry, who had done virtually nothing to alleviate the atrocious treatment of the prisoners. Meanwhile, Sir Moses himself was warned by Colonel Hodges and de Wagner, the Prussian Consul General, that in Damascus he would be murdered. Such a visit by a Jew would be interpreted as an attempt to screen the guilt of the prisoners.

Eventually on 15 August, Mr. Briggs, a British merchant, brought Sir Moses the news he had prayed for—Mehemet Ali promised to liberate the prisoners. He prepared a document for the approval and signature of the Pasha, only to receive another setback when the latter declined to sign it! Cochelet had intervened with his own weird proposal that the Pasha declare that the Jews who had *died* had committed the murders, but the Jews still in prison were innocent! Sir Moses was resolute:

'I would rather die than consent to any compromise which would cast a stain on the memory of the unhappy men who so nobly endured their dreadful sufferings. One of them died with the words of the Shema on his lips and the whole relying on the God of Israel to remove from their memories the imputation of murder.'

The alleged murder was, after all, a *ritual* murder, and for a French consul to countenance this was a far-reaching and dangerous precedent.

What was becoming daily more apparent to Sir Moses was that Christians were being more obstructive than Moslems in this case, the Catholic Church had irrevocably committed itself to the guilt of the prisoners, and the French Foreign Ministry was using the Pasha as a puppet. No reply had been forthcoming from his petition, so Sir Moses, with Crémieux, arranged another to be drawn up, this time by the consuls of the Four Powers who should present it in person to the Pasha. Sir Moses was prepared to forgo his visit and full enquiry in Damascus if the Pasha released the prisoners, recited in the firman his conviction of their innocence, his disbelief that Jews committed murder for the sake of blood in their ceremonies, and his permission for Jews who had fled their homes to return.

This compromise was to prove crucial to the success of the mission. There was little time left. If a war ensued it would deprive the prisoners of any protection at all. While they waited for a response, Sir Moses sought to check the Pasha's previous commitment to abolish slavery. He toured the slave market. This was depressing. He saw about one hundred slaves, mostly children but a few women. Girls could be purchased for 1,000 piastres (£10) and boys for 600. He witnessed two boys weeping bitterly; they had been brought from Nubia and were probably brothers. One had just been sold. The master took him away. It was unlikely that they would ever see each other again. 'Oh! the horrors of slavery!' exclaimed Sir Moses.

Two days' later, on 28 August, he went to see the Pasha and asked for an answer to the petition. At last, there was something for the mission. Mehemet Ali promised to release the prisoners, grant a firman, allow the Jews who had fled to return to their homes, and to direct Sherif Pasha to protect the Jews as he did Moslems and Christians. Although the disturbed state of Syria and the opposition of the French had prevented him from proceeding to Damascus to obtain a new trial, Sir Moses had achieved a great deal:

'Thanks to heaven, the Mission has gained something; the lives of nine innocent persons are thus preserved.'

He then attended divine service in the European synagogue.

Not everyone in Britain shared his sense of relief and achievement. A letter from 'TJC, Oxford' in *The Times* of 20 October attacked him for renouncing an investigation urgently demanded by public opinion, and for boasting the innocence of the prisoners when letters from Syria 'proved' their guilt. Sir Moses read this when in Malta in December, and in response quoted naval officers who had been in Damascus and had warned him of the dangers of going there. The substance of the naval officers' correspondence was this; they were in Damascus on 10 August—Lieutenant Shadwell and Rev. Joseph Marshall, both of H.M.S. *Castor*, and Rev. Schlientz of Malta. Marshall described the insults hurled upon the families of those in prison

'their houses broken into and plundered with impunity, jewels torn from the persons of their female relatives, young children imprisoned and tortured with starvation, the son bastinadoed before the mother's eyes to make her betray her husband's place of concealment, the most exorbitant bribes demanded to permit the common necessaries of life to pass the gates of the prison for its bruised and wretched inhabitants. There exists not at present the shadow of evidence against them.'

He advised against the practicability or prudence of Sir Moses visiting Damascus. Lieutenant Shadwell had seen the inscription in the Latin Convent of the Capuchins to Father Thomas: 'Here rest the bones of Father Tomaso of Sardinia, Capuchin missionary, murdered by the Hebrews on February 5th 1840'.

He saw the prisoners

'the tortures to which they had been subjected were of the most cruel and disgraceful nature, and some of them even too disgusting to be mentioned with propriety. There is no admissible evidence to support the charge. The only two witnesses who appeared in favour of the Jews were conveniently disposed of by being bastinadoed to death. The pillaging and extortions to which the Jewish families have been subjected affords a clue to the motives which have instigated the persecutors.'

He also thought the appearance of Sir Moses in Damascus would be highly dangerous. The Rev. Schlientz endorsed these observations.

Not everything went quite to plan about the firman. Crémieux had no support from his Government and was dependent for his diplomatic status on Sir Moses, although Crémieux was to snatch the glory by obtaining the official exoneration of the Jews from the blood libel. What happened was that, on 29 August, Loewe and Munk had gone to the Palace to collect the firman but noticed the word 'Afoo' meaning 'pardon' (that is, the Jews had been

'pardoned' for the crime committed). This was not a vindication at all. Loewe
recorded in his diary:

*'I immediately pointed it out to Negeb Effendi (one of Mehemet Ali's chief secretaries)
and said that Sir Moses would certainly not be satisfied with such an expression, as the
Jews could never even have been supposed guilty, according to the mode of proceedings which
had been taken in the case.'*

Loewe asked Munk to take the firman to Sir Moses but Munk took it to
Crémieux, who immediately went to the Palace and got the offending word
replaced with 'itlak ve tervîhh' (an honourable liberation). Sir Moses was
angered:

*'Had I known it, I should have been most indignant with the Pasha for inserting the
word, it being in complete opposition to my request, as I would never, for an instant
admit any guilt, either of the living or of the dead.'*

The Mission waited in Alexandria for news of the release of the prisoners. This
occurred on 5 September but only reached Sir Moses on 15 September. Dr.
Loewe wrote ecstatically in his diary:

*'This day is the happiest in my life. I was the fortunate messenger who brought the news
to Sir Moses that a letter had arrived, stating the liberation of the Jews at Damascus.'*

The prisoners were liberated from the crime of 'murder for religious purposes'
and returned to what was left of their homes (seven of the nine had been
crippled for life).

Sir Moses believed the whole plot had been manufactured by Thiers and the
French Government, and put into operation by a few fanatical Catholics and
the French Consul. On 27 September he confided in Louis Cohen regarding
Mehemet Ali:

*'He is no enemy to the Jews; to the fanaticism of the Catholics of Damascus and the
diabolical hatred of Ratti-Menton and some of the authorities of that city is the horrid
charge to be solely attributed.'*

On his last visit to the Pasha, the latter said he was glad to hear of the
'honourable liberation' and informed Sir Moses that Jews who had fled the city
had now returned. On 17 September Sir Moses boarded the *Leonidas*, the same
ship he and Lady Montefiore had taken on their first momentous voyage to the

Holy Land. They now embarked upon a shorter but no less momentous journey to the Sultan.

'We sang the "Song of Moses", and with joy and thanks, left the land of Egypt.'

They entered the Lazaretto, Syra five days' later, for the quarantine which Dr. Loewe explains in his diary:

'During the day we performed the ceremony called the Spoglio. After having exposed all our clothes and other effects to the air in our own room, we all quitted the rooms; in each of them some black mixture dissolved in water was placed over a chafing dish, which caused a very disagreeable smell. We were ordered to have prepared an outfit from top to toe and to leave it in the room to be fumigated. In about half an hour's time we repaired to the bath and then exchanged our things for those fumigated. The quarantine doctor came to examine our health, and particularly to see whether we had any signs of the plague.'

They arrived in Constantinople on 5 October. The following day was the Day of Atonement so the Montefiores fasted and remained in synagogue. Sir Moses asked Lord Ponsonby, with whom he dined on 15 October, for an audience with the Sultan, to thank him for his justice to Jews and obtain a declaration of protection for them in his Empire. Lord Ponsonby introduced him to Rechid Pasha, the Grand Vizier, who arranged this audience with the Sultan for 28 October.

'Our cavalcade consisted of one carriage with four horses, and one with two horses, six kávásses or police officers, eight men carrying large wax torches, two horsemen with each coach, a sedan chair with each coach. I wore my full uniform. The streets were crowded; many of the Jews had illuminated their houses. We reached the Palace in rather less than an hour. We found in the courtyard a large guard of honour, who presented arms. We were shown into a handsome drawing-room, furnished in the European style. Rechid Pasha entered. We were soon joined by Rizá Pasha, and all were served with coffee and pipes, the mouthpieces and bowls of the latter being richly embellished with diamonds. We crossed a garden about sixty yards in length, and entered a handsome marble hall;

Sir Moses submits an address in Constantinople to Sultan Abdul Medjid of Turkey in 1840.

having descended a grand staircase, likewise of marble, we entered into the presence chamber. The Sultan was seated on a sofa, clad in his cloak of state which was fastened at the neck with two large clasps of the finest diamonds. He was a good looking young man, and appeared about twenty-six years of age, though in reality but nineteen. After having received some courteous signs of welcome from him, I delivered the speech. "Under your righteous direction the oppressor was laid low, the designs of the wicked made known, and the innocent delivered."'

The Sultan was prepared to grant him what he requested:

'I have been affected by the events which have taken place in Damascus, but I have endeavoured to offer some satisfaction to the Israelitish nation, by giving orders that justice should be done in the affair of Rhodes. The Israelitish nation shall always have, from me, the same protection and enjoy the same advantages as all other subjects of my Empire. I will grant the deputation the firman they have asked. I know, gentlemen, how to appreciate the pure philanthropy which has led you to this capital.'

Leaving the room in which he met the Sultan, a room furnished in European style with an English carpet, Sir Moses was honoured:

The Firman.

'We were again served, after the audience, in the lower room of the palace with sherbet in elegant glasses. A military band played during the greater part of the time we were at the Palace. We found the streets still more crowded than when we went; not a window in the whole street through which we passed but was filled with female faces.'

Back at the house where they were staying he was delighted to share with Lady Montefiore 'the complete success of our Mission.'

On Saturday evening at 10 p.m. on 7 November, the original firman, signed by the Sultan, was brought to Sir Moses. It was beautifully written on thick parchment and enclosed in a coloured satin bag. It proclaimed that the charges against Jews using human blood was calumny, that they would be protected and defended on the same basis of equality as other subjects, and molestation of them in their religion was prohibited. It implied the abolition of torture in trials, a diplomatic coup for Sir Moses, who informed the Board of Deputies:

'The Firman will be productive of lasting benefit to our people. In the East it is as much appreciated as were the Acts for the Repeal of the Catholic Disabilities and the Test and Corporation Acts at home. It is, indeed, the "Magna Carta" for the Jews in the Turkish dominions.'

The Firman was experienced as a significant victory. Jews would be accorded the same status as fellow subjects, admitted to full equality of citizenship. It was symbolic of the progress of toleration, in Sir Moses' judgement. On the back of a printed translation of the firman, he commented to fellow-philanthropist Isaac Lyon Goldsmid:

'This document has been hailed with universal joy by our co-religionists here and it is looked upon as the great Charter of their liberties; and I hope it will teach a lesson to other Governments of true liberality and lead to the realisation of your wishes in the repeal of those obnoxious laws which exclude us from office and power at home. I look upon the Firman as a great step in advance and one eminently calculated to raise all in the East possessing our religion to a perfect equality with the Turks and thus give a new impetus to that thrust for mental and moral improvement which has distinguished our people at home.'

Of all his activities and devotion to the fate and fortune of his people, Sir Moses would be best remembered as the person who 'resolved' the most sensational cause célèbre of the mid-nineteenth century, the Damascus blood libel.

Before he left Constantinople there was another vital task to perform, and one which became a life-long commitment to him. This was Jewish education.

He believed that Jews would be emancipated according to local circumstances. They had to assimilate themselves by learning the local language while preserving their own religious institutions. For six days in Constantinople he devoted himself to this issue and drew up a proclamation recommending an order to teach all children the Turkish language. Representatives of Jewish congregations later thanked him for introducing this study of Turkish language and its literature in their schools, and agreed that it would raise them in the estimation of Moslems.

Rechid Pasha acknowledged this:

'If you had done nothing more than this in Constantinople you should consider your-self amply compensated for the trouble and fatigue you have undergone. In advising your brethren to acquire a knowledge of the Turkish language you have been instru-mental in enabling them to raise themselves to some of the highest offices in the Empire.'

Meanwhile, living conditions were wretched for many. Sir Moses visited Kháskoey to distribute money among the poor but concluded that he had *never* witnessed so much poverty and distress. Dr. Loewe depicted the scene in his own diary:

'We left Synagogue with the intention of distributing the money among the poor, but people came in crowds. Blind, old, and sick men were sitting on the ground and crowds of poor rushed over them. Sir M. after having given to 30 poor persons, was obliged to give up that pleasing occupation and hand the money to the leader of the Synagogue. Seven soldiers and two officers were obliged to make room for us to proceed.'

However, one event symbolised the mission at the end—an emotional meeting with Isaac Piciotto (the Austrian subject in Damascus who had brought the Affair to international attention). He shed tears on meeting Sir Moses and expressed great gratitude for his intervention.

On 9 November Sir Moses was on his travels again, landing at Smyrna where he left Greek translations of the firman. In Dr. Loewe's diary of 1840 the atmosphere is captured:

'We went on shore in the Captain's boat and landed near the Jewish quarter. Crowds of people flocked around us to see Sir Moses and Lady Montefiore, their liberators. We went into the large Synagogue, said Minha prayers and proceeded to the house of the Haham Sezura.'

Hearing that the Pasha was now contenting himself with vice-regal power in Egypt, Sir Moses remarked

'if the Sultan allowed Mehemet Ali to retain Egypt, he would not suffer Syria to remain quiet for twelve months, but would excite insurrections.'

He also heard of the reception of the firman by Jews—joy and prayers for the Sultan and Sir Moses and in Malta he gave Colonel Charles Churchill, who was going to Damascus, copies of the Sultan's firman for representatives of the Jewish community there. Removal of the libellous epitaph on the Capuchins' tomb was the next objective, and the destination Rome, in the hope of an audience with the Pope. On his journey, in Naples, Baron Charles de Rothschild gained him an interview with the Pope's Nuncio, who complimented Sir Moses on his success, adding that he was an excellent ambassador. Meanwhile at a meeting with the French Ambassador, Sir Moses was advised to notify the French Government of Ratti-Menton's conduct but not to 'publish it to the world.'

From Naples, the Montefiores travelled in their carriage to Rome. There he had an interview with Mr. Aubin, the acting agent for the British Government, who announced that the Pope's circle believed the Jews had murdered Father

Thomas. The likelihood of the Pope receiving Sir Moses faded, but it was the end of the year, a time for reflection:

> *'It has been a year of much anxiety, fatigue and danger to Lady Montefiore and myself, but thanks to the God of our Fathers, we trust its fruits will be productive of much good to the children, not only in the East, but in the West as well.'*

A Signor Bruti on 1 January 1841 suggested to Sir Moses that the petition might be accepted by some Capuchins if it was accompanied by gifts of money. Sir Moses retorted that he had given no money in the execution of his Mission and he would not in Rome either. Bruti 'forgot' to impart this message to Cardinal Agostino Riverola, the head of the Capuchin Order, who insinuated that the firman had been obtained by Rothschild's fortune. (Sir Moses answered that he would never attempt to obtain justice by bribery.) Riverola was, however, impressed by the firman and 'sanctioned' the removal of the epitaph to Father Thomas. Sir Moses committed to his diary his hope that

> *'with patience and perseverance I may succeed in getting the inscription removed.'*

He had both qualities in abundance but the inscription stayed.

Cardinal Riverola promised to advise the removal of the stone from the Convent but could not order its removal because the Convent was under the protection of the French authorities. The next task for Sir Moses was an interview with Louis Philippe. On that journey Lady Montefiore became seriously ill, with numbness in her hand and arm and pain in her head, and they had a serious accident on the road from Genoa to Savona. They did not reach Paris until 18 February. He was going into the lion's den. Thiers had taken a prominent part in the Damascus Affair and the Turkish Sultan had just humiliated France in a political struggle. Sir Moses was sure that the King was too great a lover of justice to refuse his request. He got his interview and presented the firman:

> *'I was so fatigued that I could eat no dinner, but dressed myself in my uniform. I went to the Palace. Lord Granville came in and we were immediately conducted into the presence of the King. I then offered to the King the translation of the Hatti-Sherif (firman); he accepted it of me in a most gracious manner, said he was happy to receive it, and enquired if I had been at Damascus.'*

Back in England on 26 February, after eight months' absence, the Montefiores were greeted with services in synagogues praising their exertions abroad in the cause of suffering humanity and the vindication of their religious tenets. Jewish communities throughout Europe, America and the Far East sent testimonials and congratulations. The Board of Deputies presented them with an elaborately executed testimonial in the shape of a silver centrepiece; the firmans were celebrated in verse and prose. The Mission had vindicated the technique of the shtadlan, the intercessor, who possessed the gifts of diplomacy and discretion with tenacity. Sir Moses' fame spread among the scattered Jewish communities of the world. He was becoming the principal spokesman.

On 3 March he thanked Lord Palmerston for his assistance, and three weeks later presented a copy of the firman to the Queen. Three months later she granted him bearers for his coat of arms, an honour which was unique and had to be specially granted. He had not only protected Jews abroad. He had exhibited that image of British humanitarianism, which was sometimes difficult to substantiate in other parts of the Empire. His mission inaugurated official or semi-official international Jewish delegations at important international gatherings to defend Jewish interests. This united action of Jews had proved that, despite their political and cultural and even religious divisions, they had a common bond. In concerting political, financial and moral assistance to a far-flung community, a precedent had been created for the political co-operation that emerged among Jews half a century later. After 1840 the word 'Damascus' became a beacon, a symbol of a new struggle for Jewish recognition by governments, particularly political emancipation. It taught Jews the value of solidarity in a cause and the necessity of a common united front. Sir Moses' straightforward approach surmounted all the intrigues in the Eastern imbroglio between governments, consuls and the ramifications in international relations.

The outcome was also a triumph for Palmerston, an impressive tactical victory even if the strategic problem and Russian ambitions remained. The crisis confirmed his distrust of the Pasha and engaged his sympathy with the plight of the Jews in Mediterranean lands. He envisaged a Syria populated by rich Jews from Europe under British protection to add to the stability and prosperity of the area, and to act as a barrier against further conquests by the Pasha. Since the opening of the Consulate in Jerusalem in 1839, the British Government had sought to further its interests in the Middle East; support of Jewish communities was part of that strategy.

The Damascus Affair had other ramifications. In April 1847 a new accusation was brought against Jews in Damascus when a boy went missing (he reappeared in Baalbeck). What had happened to the guarantees of 1840? Had Sir Moses been too optimistic, too reliant on the promulgation of a firman? He asked Lord Palmerston to assist him in gaining a private audience with Louis Philippe, because the superstition had again been reinforced by the French Consulate's agent, Baudin, who had accused the Jews to the Ottoman Governor, Sefata Pasha. The latter, seemingly unacquainted with the firman, had imprisoned several Jews on suspicion.

Fortunately, Sir Moses could now consult Guizot, who wrote to the Consul at Damascus to denounce this unsubstantiated libel. On 9 August Sir Moses' audience with the King took place at the Palace of the Tuileries. He was conducted through a splendid picture gallery and several large apartments to a room. Louis Philippe entered and greeted him: 'I am very happy to see you, Sir Moses.' The outcome was satisfactory; the consular officers were censured and, after long correspondence with the Turkish authorities, the imprisoned Jews were set free. Although Guizot tried to reassure Sir Moses that the French Government regarded the libel as false and calumnious (and French agents too enlightened to abet it), Palmerston believed that the French authorities in Damascus had precipitated and encouraged the charge against the Jews, as they had in 1840.

On his third visit to the Holy Land in 1848, Sir Moses once again endeavoured to get the Father Thomas epitaph removed, since the Jewish community at Damascus had expressed their fears to him:

'on account of this epitaph the feelings of hatred and revenge entertained by Christians towards Jews may be perpetuated through coming generations. Whoever sees the inscription is filled with hatred and indignation against Israel.'

Arriving in Damascus on 3 July, he found the Church of the Capuchins, where, to his great sorrow, he saw the epitaph. It was still there on Sir Moses' fourth visit to Jerusalem in 1855, so Lord Cowley, the British Ambassador, was informed of Sir Moses' desire to petition the Emperor, Louis Napoleon, for a letter to the French Consul at Damascus to secure its removal.

The unexpected culmination to this twenty-year mission happened in 1860. In July 1860, the Syrian Christians were attacked by the Druze of Mount Lebanon so Sir Moses proposed in *The Times* a British Syrian Relief

Committee to help the homeless and destitute. He began the fund with a donation of £200 and became the Chairman of the Executive Committee. Insinuations flew around that he and Crémieux were actuated by a desire to expiate the ritual murder of Father Thomas, but the Druse got there first. During the disturbance at Damascus, the Church of the Capuchins was destroyed and with it the notorious inscription. Not that this ended persecutions. Within a month, the Jewish community was entreating Sir Moses to intercede because of allegations that they were aiding Moslems to kill Christians. *Ten years later* these allegations were revamped in a letter to *The Times* by E. H. Palmer and C. F. Tyrwhitt Drake, following another massacre by Moslems of Christians. They castigated the Jews who in 1860

> '*distinguished themselves by standing at the doors of their houses, and voluntarily offering lemonade to refresh the Mahommedans, hot and weary with the slaughter of the Christians, and who, in many well authenticated instances, offered aid and concealment to the terror-stricken Christians and then brought in the Turks to murder them.*'

In a dignified reply, which the letter hardly merited, Sir Moses regretted that gentlemen so intelligent should be so ready to give credence to any absurd rumours and that the charges against the Jews were 'devoid of truth'.

The blood libel would not die. In April 1882, in Hungary, a fourteen-year-old girl Esther Solymossi disappeared. Jews were subsequently accused of her murder to use blood for Passover. It was back to Damascus—intrigues, machinations, personal malice, religious hatred, national prejudice, ignorant superstition, Jews imprisoned, Jewish houses plundered, tortures, a trial and eventual release for lack of evidence. Nearly 98 years old, Sir Moses corresponded with Count Tisza, (Minister President of the Imperial and Royal House of Representatives in Budapest) concerning the allegations that European Jews in 1840 had offered large sums of money to Austrian and French Consulates in Damascus to gain their favourable services, and that the accused had been liberated by act of grace by the Pasha:

> '*no other means were used to obtain the liberation of the Jews in Damascus than those of justice and truth. Mehemet Ali granted them freedom and rest (itlâk î tarwich). This was no act of grace but of justice and it is with the feeling of the greatest indignation that I reject the accusation brought by the author of that interpellation against the Jews of Europe.*'

The Montefiore Testimonial, presented in 1843.

5. A VOYAGE TO RUSSIA

After the Damascus Affair Sir Moses had become a beacon of hope for Jews throughout the world. Letters addressed to him at the Board of Deputies can still be seen, from people who described the appalling plight of Jews in Russia and Poland, urging him to intercede on their behalf with the Russian Government and to proceed at once to St. Petersburg to make known their cause to the Emperor. Sir Moses announced to the Board in September 1842 his invitation to St. Petersburg to discuss the new system of education with Count Ouvaroff. The Russian Government believed that their 'enlightened' plan was opposed by 'the bigotry and ignorance' of the Jewish population, so they appealed in flattering terms to Sir Moses for his co-operation:

> 'You, Sir, enjoy the fullest confidence of the Russian Jews; your name is uttered with the most profound veneration by them.'

Through his presence and advice the Russian Government thought the scheme would be made acceptable to them.

At first, Sir Moses considered Ouvaroff's ideas on secular education should be evaluated as a blessing for Jews (and Max Lilienthal of Riga had intimated as much in his letter requesting this visit to St. Petersburg). Although other petitions from Russia informed him that the new educational provisions were

The map used by Sir Moses on the visit to St. Petersburg.

not without complications, and might be a scheme for proselytisation, in October and November 1842 further petitions from America and Western Europe entreated Sir Moses to accept Ouvaroff's invitation. He consulted the Russian Consul-General, Chevalier Benkhausen, who recommended a meeting with Brunnow, the Czar's ambassador in London, who made the necessary inquiries for the intended journey. There would be strict procedures involved. He advised Sir Moses to travel directly to St. Petersburg and speak to the Czar, not to acquire information or allow rapturous welcomes from Jewish communities en route. Sir Moses had intended to visit Polish cities first, and had he done so, his audience with the Czar and Ministers would have been buttressed with specific knowledge of Jewish grievances, but this proposed trip in 1842 did not materialise.

Instead, on a brief visit to England, the Czar met Lord Aberdeen. Sir Moses did everything possible to obtain an interview, but it was too short a visit to arrange a deputation. He had to make do with an Address from the Board of Deputies to Brunnow, who advised Sir Moses to write to Ouvaroff soliciting an abrogation of the decree deporting Jews from border areas. He thought it was a 'bad measure' but the Russian Minister of Justice justified it as an act of mercy relieving Jews of the temptation to smuggle goods across the border.

Then, in 1844, the Czar ordered the Minister of the Interior to present him with a detailed analysis of the situation and property of Jews in frontier towns and villages before the ukase was put into full operation. By November the ukase was being implemented and a special delegate arrived from Poland to entreat Sir Moses to intercede. A decision was made to go to St. Petersburg when he had completed his term of office as Sheriff of Kent. Baron Brunnow gave him letters of introduction to Count Nesselrode and other Russian Ministers, and advised him to travel as an English gentleman not as the representative of the Board of Deputies. He reiterated that the Czar's objective was not to convert Jews but render them 'more useful subjects', a phrase on the lips of every Minister in St. Petersburg. Brunnow had misgivings about the proposed visit, one time recommending Sir Moses not to go, another time pleading that if he was determined to go 'to keep as quiet as possible . . .' Sir Moses had no intention of compromising his mission but promised, as he had in 1842, not to receive deputations or countenance ovations from Jewish communities until he had seen the Czar and his Ministers.

Accompanied by his wife, he left England on 1 March 1846, with letters of introduction from Lord Aberdeen and Sir Robert Peel to Lord Bloomfield, British Ambassador in St. Petersburg. It was their first visit to Eastern Europe. At the Russian Embassy in Berlin, Mr. Fonton warned them of bad weather ahead and almost impassable roads which would prevent carriage-travel. Characteristically, Sir Moses could not be dissuaded. From Berlin they travelled to Königsberg, Tilsit and Mitau. They suffered from the biting cold, heavy snows and pitted roads. The journey was long and tedious. Frequently they were compelled to travel all night. Alarmed by the howling of hungry packs of wolves, they had to keep a gong perpetually sounding to frighten them away. This was only the first of many hazards:

'When we reached Obay, on the south side of the Dwina, opposite Riga at 10.35, we found the river still covered with ice, but in a weak and dangerous condition. Our carriages were deemed too heavy to be passed over; but after considerable hesitation, they were allowed to be conveyed across, though at a great expense and at our own risk. The wheels were taken off, as well as all the luggage, and they were then placed on sledges and drawn by men to the opposite side of the river. At 1.30 p.m. we all walked across. We

Winter in Russia.

had great difficulty in walking, the ice was wet and slippery, with numerous dangerous holes. Not two minutes before we passed, a man fell into one of these holes, and was drowned.'

Sir Moses commented later 'It was impossible to express the alarm we felt in crossing.'

On his journey to St. Petersburg, and, in accordance with the agreement with Brunnow, he avoided deputations from Jewish communities. There were many appearance of these but Sir Moses kept his word. They trudged on, from Riga to Narva to Jamburg:

'Snow had again fallen heavily. We found the ice in such a bad state that grave fears were entertained as to the possibility of crossing the River Lugu. The officer in charge repeatedly refused to allow us to cross.'

Next day,

'The carriages were safely put on a large barge, and soon launched into the stream, but when in the middle it struck on some large stones, and they were in the greatest peril. The barge remained for nearly an hour fixed to one spot. After great exertions on the part of the soldiers, it was got off.'

The officer then conducted Sir Moses and Lady Montefiore into his own boat:

'We were towed across, though not without some danger from the ice which was driving down the current in great masses, and which our boatman found great difficulty in avoiding. Had they struck it must have proved fatal.'

They landed safely. At Opolje, the roads were so rutted and icy they were compelled to leave their carriages. They walked through the snow and eventually arrived 'dreadfully fatigued' at Ischerkowitz. With a little open carriage placed on a sledge and drawn by two horses, they travelled in the freezing cold from there to Kaskowa. The following day they reached Stretna. The road from there to St. Petersburg was in excellent condition, 'well macadamised' because on either side of the road were the country houses of the nobility. They reached the Hotel de Prusse in St. Petersburg on 1 April.

Life for Jews in Eastern Europe in the 1840s was oppressive and restricted. Czar Nicholas I (1825–1855) had sought, under the banner 'Orthodoxy, Autocracy and Nationalism', to created homogeneity in the Russian Empire,

An open carriage on a sledge – the only means of travel.

and to undermine Jewish independence. He had introduced a ukase (decree) in 1827 which re-interpreted the conscription law. By it Jewish children were drafted into the army or navy from the age of 12, then at 18 they would begin the normal 25 years' service. Through abductions such forcible recruitment had resulted in tragic family ordeals, some conversions to Christianity and many suicides. For the Czar army service succeeded in reducing the number of devout Jews. A new law was promulgated in 1835 to remove 'all inducements to indolence and illegal pursuits', and used to expel Jews from specific cities. Further restrictions were enforced; Jews were forbidden to employ Christians or use the Yiddish language in public documents. Censorship of literature was accompanied by the closure of printing presses and the ransacking of private libraries. Even when Siberia was opened to Jewish colonisation and re-settlement as farmers, officials confiscated the equipment and seed required.

A decade of onerous conscription, expulsion decrees and harsh taxes failed to integrate Russian Jews. By 1840 the Czar was faced with three million Jews who remained traditional in religion and occupation. Another strategy was now employed. He instructed Count Kisseleff, the Minister for Jewish Affairs, to resolve Jewish separatism and 'religious fanaticism'. The Talmud was castigated as the inspiration for the exclusiveness, blamed for fostering contempt towards other faiths and for implying that the Empire was a place of captivity. Since the Talmud was the basis of Jewish institutions, schools and local self-government, a new secular education was to be instigated. Abandonment of the Talmud was written into this by Count Ouvaroff, Minister of Public Instruction. He approached Max Lilienthal of Riga to devise a new Jewish school system as a preliminary for 'future emancipation'; in practice the Czar placed Jewish communities under Russian administration. Another ukase expelled them from the densely-populated Russian frontier zone bordering Germany and Austria. Ostensibly a law to prevent smuggling, it fragmented thousands of Jewish communities and left them destitute. Most professions were closed to them. New taxes were imposed on Jewish peddlers and small tradesmen. The only means left for self-defence were the hevras (voluntary self-help associations).

What Russian Jews required was civil emancipation, less restrictions and wider economic opportunities. Lilienthal could not get these reassurances, and by the time Sir Moses reached St. Petersburg he had emigrated to America. Eradication of study of the Talmud and encouragement of Crown schools (by exempting students from military conscription) failed, but the oppressions intensified. Before his arrival in Russia in 1846, Sir Moses had been aware of the deterioration in the treatment of Russian Jews. He had received a detailed report on St. Petersburg from Mr. Gilbert, a representative of the Imperial Continental Gas Company, who had toured the city in 1827, and throughout the 1830s he had frequent contact with Baron Brunnow. He had appealed through him for the withdrawal or postponement of the decrees which threatened Jewish communities.

The journey to St. Petersburg from London had taken exactly one month. Sir Moses' first call was to the British Ambassador, Bloomfield. Having come to see the four central figures in the Russian Government, Count Nesselrode, Count Ouvaroff, Count Kisseleff and the Czar, he was hopeful that 'good will' negotiations would change the policy of the Government and reverse the deleterious effect of the ukase. He was not prepared for the accusations levelled against the Jews at his meetings.

Nesselrode was the first to castigate the Russian Jews. He claimed that the cream of the Jews were in Western Europe, whereas those in the Russian Empire were 'engaged in low traffic and contraband pursuits'. Sir Moses expressed deep regrets on hearing such allegations but said he had come on the matter of Jewish schools and the repeal of the ukase. He had responded to a particular emergency and was unprepared for the Ministers' criticisms.

This was more apparent at his meeting with Ouvaroff. The new school system was a conversionary mechanism but Ouvaroff was not going to say so. Having invited Sir Moses to exert his influence in the promotion of the secular education of Jews, he assured him that the ukase for schools was designed for their 'happiness'. As Nesselrode had put it, and Ouvaroff repeated, it would make them more useful members of society. He assured Sir Moses that the Government had plans for more liberal treatment but Jews first had to prepare themselves, especially those who were orthodox and believed in the Talmud. Sir Moses defended the Talmud, but Ouvaroff retorted that Jews had to be 'educated' before full facilities to gain a living were given to them, while the Government's new plan to treat them with toleration would take 'perhaps a century' to make any appreciable difference. Sir Moses requested that they should at least be relieved from the anxiety and suffering caused by the ukase which removed them from frontier towns, but Ouvaroff reiterated Nesselrode's conviction that the 35 mile ban removed the temptations of smuggling. In reply to Ouvaroff's comment that the responsibility lay with Jews to improve themselves and attend schools, Sir Moses asserted that only fear of attempts at conversion made them hesitate.

Sir Moses received in audience by Czar Nicholas I, 1846.

Sir Moses with Czar Nicholas I.

The white gloves worn during the audience with the Czar.

Czar Nicholas I granted him an audience on 9 April. Sir Moses attached the greatest importance to this, and in the Judith. Lady Montefiore College preserved the pair of white gloves he wore when he shook hands with the Czar. In honour of the occasion, the Palace guard for the day was composed of Jewish soldiers, 100,000 of whom were in the army. Sir Moses was very impressed by the welcome and flattered by such acts of courtesy, even though this did not affect the eventual implementation of the ukase. Procuring the revocation of this proved difficult, but he tried:

'I made the strongest appeal in my power for the general alteration of all laws and edicts that pressed heavily on the Jews under His Majesty's sway.'

He thanked the Czar for intimating that his presence in the city might be beneficial to Russian Jews in terms of the organisation of schools, and said he wanted Jews to be given the opportunity to prove themselves loyal, useful, industrious and honourable citizens. 'If they are like you', the Czar replied.

The problem was that Russian Jews were not like Sir Moses. Their Government thought funds from Western Europe for the education of Jews would relieve them of their responsibility, and while Sir Moses believed the condition of Jews would be ameliorated as a result of his meetings, he had not vouched for the incipient anti-semitism in the Government. This was not directed at him, though. He was treated as a distinguished private individual, a guest of the Czar. State carriages were placed at his disposal and a Government official was in constant attendance.

Meeting the Jewish soldiers gave him most satisfaction. On 11 April the Minister of War escorted him through mud and rain for two miles to the service in the soldiers' synagogue at the barracks. For the occasion, the synagogue was beautifully decorated at the expense of the Czar. Sir Moses attended a second service six days later, when the soldiers informed him that his arrival had been beneficial for them; the officers had treated them better since then. He discovered that they could observe their religion and live in barracks with their wives and children. Years later, in the Crimean War, he visited Russian Jewish prisoners at Sheerness and thanked the British Government for treating humanely those taken prisoner at Kertsch.

Better late than never, Sir Moses went to the office of the Secret Police, since it was customary for visitors to St. Petersburg to pay a visit there! Some might stay longer, but he had an appointment with Count Kisseleff, Minister for Jewish Affairs, who launched an attack on Russian Jews. They were, he asserted, 'fanatics' praying for the coming Messiah and their return to the Holy Land; their belief in the Talmud was the cause of their degraded position; they starved themselves all week in order to have candles and fish for the Sabbath. Sir Moses carefully corrected the errors in these accusations but Kisseleff showed him a ukase which compelled Jews to adopt an active occupation or be punished as vagrants. He offered Sir Moses the option of transporting '10,000 or more to Palestine or elsewhere'. Having imputed the characteristics of Russian Jews as fanaticism, smuggling, laziness, strange customs and dress, he told him that the new plan for Jews was 'conciliatory', and, echoing the other Ministers, that he only cared that Jews were useful citizens!

Sir Moses was unusually optimistic about the outcome of his visit:

'I am satisfied that the Jews will be better off in consequence of our visit to this city. Praise be to God alone!'

He recognised land cultivation and establishment of manufactories as the solution to the poverty of Jewish communities, but the most useful aspect of his visit was obtaining facilities to travel throughout the Jewish Pale of Settlement to gather information and collect any documents relating to the life of Jews, in order to prepare reports to the Ministers refuting the criticisms levelled against Jews. His research was about to begin. Further travels ensued:

'Regiza . . . We find the post stations get worse as we proceed, both in respect to cleanliness and comfort. Last night there was no bread, no beer, wine or spirits, and very bad water, and beds out of the question. We have slept on sofas since we left St. Petersburg, with the greater part of our clothes on, being covered with our cloaks. It is indeed roughing it.'

On 29 April they reached Wilna, and received a rapturous welcome from the local Jewish community. Wilna, the capital of Lithuania, with a Jewish settlement since the thirteenth century, was in 1846 the foremost centre of Jewish culture. The Montefiores spent eleven days there. Count Ouvaroff had given a letter of introduction for the local Inspector of Public Instruction, and Count Nesselrode a letter to the local Governor. The latter attributed the unhappy state of Jews in Wilna to desperate poverty. He proposed colonisation as the remedy, and when Sir Moses heard complaints from Jewish families expelled from villages, the Governor protested that Jews did not have to leave the villages but only had to discontinue selling brandy.

Sir Moses utilised this visit for his report. He met the local nobility, inspected colleges and schools, visited the Jewish Hospital, the infant school and the Orphan Asylum. He exhorted pupils in schools to study Russian language and literature, and met leading members of the Jewish community. They stated that the Government would not permit them to have land or employ them as labourers, and answered the allegations made by the Czar's Ministers. Dr. Loewe described the emotional scene:

'The representatives of three millions of loyal subjects of the Emperor of Russia pleaded their cause and vindicated their innocence against the most serious charges brought against them and their religious tenets by the Ministers of the Empire. I repeatedly noticed tears rolling down the cheeks of the venerable elders of the community. Sir Moses and Lady Montefiore themselves could hardly suppress their emotion.'

Having sent hundreds of bottles of wine and cakes to the hospitals, Sir Moses and his wife left Wilna. As he stepped into his carriage, he declared:

'I leave you, but my heart will ever remain with you. When my brethren suffer, I feel it painfully; when they have reason to weep, my eyes shed tears.'

Hundreds of these people followed the carriage for miles. In Wilcomir Sir Moses was told that of 500 Jewish families, a quarter had died of destitution the previous year, and in Kowno, he discovered that Jews only acquired two-thirds the pay other workers received. Months later, he received news from Kowno that the Czar had issued a ukase permitting Jews to remain in the town free from molestation. Twenty-three years after his visit, he noticed a report in *The Times* of great distress among peasants in Kowno and sent £100 for the sufferers of all religious denominations. From Kowno they journeyed to Warsaw, where further scenes of enthusiasm at their arrival occurred. Sir Moses was greeted in Wilna, Kowno, and Warsaw as the intercessor with magical powers. His portrait began to appear in Jewish homes all over Russia and Poland, such did he raise the morale of Jews. He listened to these communities, gave them encouragement and hope, and prepared his reports from their experiences.

The British Ambassador at St. Petersburg, Bloomfield, had given him a letter of introduction to Colonel du Plat, British Consul at Warsaw. Through him Sir Moses discussed the condition of Jews with the Minister of the Interior,

Military Governor and Minister of Foreign Affairs. They argued that Jews would not cultivate the land, although the Jews he met claimed that they could not get permission to cultivate the land, Prince Paskiewitz, the Viceroy, being unwilling to give them any privileges at all. Sir Moses' message, which he reinforced on subsequent travels abroad, was that Jews could gain the good-will of these rulers by adopting the speech, customs and dress of their surroundings. Mr. Posener, head of the Hassidim Jewish community, promised him they would comply with the Government and change Polish for German costume, but they were not enthusiastic about it, and, harassed and threatened, clung tenaciously to deep-rooted ideas and habits. Two years later a plan drawn up by Posener for tenancy, farms and estates was submitted to Sir Moses and forwarded to the Russian Ambassador. This was one positive outcome of Sir Moses' assessment to the Prince that Jews wished to purchase land and cultivate it, and an improvement on the situation during his visit to Warsaw:

'I was pained to witness how some labour for a bit of bread. There were thousands of them on the roads breaking stones, and truly happy when they could get even that humiliating employment.'

Sir Robert Peel evinced a keen interest in this mission to Russia. On his return in mid-June 1846 Sir Moses informed Peel that the ukase had been abrogated and he thought Jews would gain the right to acquire and cultivate land. On 28 June, Peel had some information for Sir Moses. The Queen had conferred upon him his baronetcy, partly to help him in his campaigns for Jews abroad. The honour bestowed upon him was immediately justified, with his three reports on his findings in Jewish communities. He confronted the accusations made against them and offered remedies for restrictions placed upon them. These documents, completed in November 1846, were unpublished during the Czar's lifetime. They detailed in moderate terms the hardships for Jews and recommendations for removal of disabilities and oppressive measures. They formed an appeal on moral grounds which at least compelled the Russian Government to be more cautious in their treatment of Jews. By persuasion and facts he hoped to alter the preconceived views of the Russian authorities.

In his first report to Count Kisseleff, on the state of Jews in Russia, he prefaced his analysis by pointing out that Jews had never been connected with plots against the Government. He accepted that Jews should be useful to society and any who had dealt in contraband goods should be treated as delinquents. However, they had legitimate grievances, which he enumerated. Expulsion from frontier cities and towns had forced them into destitution. Merchants had no permission to travel to foreign countries or import from them, and could not visit St. Petersburg on commercial business. The Kahals had been abolished. Jews were forbidden to employ Christian servants or settle as agriculturists near Christians. They were prohibited from keeping brewhouses and could not be promoted in the army or navy if they distinguished themselves. Most Jews were common labourers or mechanics but were not allowed to pursue their work in the new settlements of Siberia and Kherson. He believed that the restoration of equal rights with other subjects would dispel the existing despondency among Jews, the majority of whom lived in extreme misery. To the Emperor he pleaded:

'raise the fallen, relieve the oppressed, cheer the desolate. They are ready to culti-vate the land, they are prepared to undertake any work however laborious; they wish to establish manufactories (and) to cultivate their minds by the study of science and

Testimonial 1846.

literature. Be assured that poverty, restriction, and disproportioned taxation have alone prevented them from effecting these objects.'

His separate report to Count Kisseleff on the state of Jews in Poland tabulated similar injustices. Jews constituted one quarter of Poland and yet were excluded from living in some cities and towns. Sometimes confined to particular streets, unable to have houses near main routes, they were prohibited from settling within three miles of the frontier. They could not employ apprentices or work with a Christian master, could not lease or own agricultural land, had to pay an excessive tax for kosher food, could not bring their goods or products into Warsaw, were accused of defrauding the Government of excise and customs, and could not bequeath wealth to their children. There were even more restrictions; prohibition from the professions of chemist, architect or lawyer; no promotion in the army or navy; blame for their situation on their separatist religion. They were unjustly accused of aversion to manual labour (when there were more Jewish labourers in proportion to their numbers than any other group), and of wearing anti-social costume (when most had adopted European-style clothing). Sir Moses systematically answered all the accusations, and made the simple plea that they should not be deprived of equal rights.

The third report offered his observations on Jewish education. He thanked the Government for promoting education and for not being antagonistic towards the Jewish faith. Although this was partly wishful thinking, and courtesy, the report was a defence of the ethical and spiritual principles of Judaism, and an appeal for the educational improvement of Jews under the Government's auspices. He reiterated their sincere attachment, obedience and loyalty to the Government, and, at the same time, praised the values of the Talmud and elucidated its contents. From his visits to Jewish schools he had discovered that most pupils could read and write Hebrew, Russian and German, although no one taught Russian in the Talmud Tora schools. He found that opposition to state schools was because they feared that children would abjure their faith. He was sure that there could be resolutions of these educational difficulties. His recommendations were concise. Jews should manage their Hebrew theological schools and appoint their own teachers for science and literature. No convert from Judaism should be appointed as a teacher in their schools, and since this was an issue of educational autonomy, all Hebrew books taken by the police from Hebrew libraries and collections by private individuals should be returned.

These three reports were sent to Lord Bloomfield at St. Petersburg, forwarded to the Ministers, and presented to the Czar. Ouvaroff replied that this was the beginning of a new era in the education of Jews, yet within a year, the education scheme had failed and he had resigned. Hopes that any substantial changes in the Russian Government's attitude would result from the mission and the reports were doomed to disappointment. Sir Moses' dedication did not bear fruit at the time, but some benefits for Russian Jews in the 1850s and 1860s emerged. The new Czar from 1855 was Alexander II. Acclaimed 'Czar-Liberator', he promised equal justice, tolerance, humanity and education for every citizen of the Empire. For a few years, press censorship was relaxed, foreign travel-restrictions removed, universities opened to all, and military service reduced to six years. The Western judicial system was introduced and in 1861 came the emancipation of the peasants. By a Government decree of 1865, Jewish merchants, skilled artisans and university graduates were permitted to move into the Russian interior. Quasi-emancipation for wealthier Russian Jews had arrived, and on his next visit to Russia in 1872 Sir Moses observed that 12,000 Jews had been able to settle in St. Petersburg. No one in the West predicted what was to happen to Jewish life in Russia in the 1880s.

6. FURTHER VISITS TO THE HOLY LAND

with extracts from Sir Moses' Diary of July and August 1855

Sir Moses visited the Holy Land seven times—in 1827, 1839, 1848, 1855, 1857, 1866 and finally in 1875 when he was over ninety years of age. He and Lady Montefiore had returned from the first journey inspired, and immediately began to organise funds for educational institutions there, but had to wait eleven years before they could venture again to the Land of Promise. Sir Moses prepared for the second visit by resigning from his position as President of the London Committee of Deputies of British Jews. On 1 November 1838 the Montefiores left London in their travelling carriage. In France they encountered heavy snowfalls and icy roads. Sir Moses commented:

'I certainly would not recommend this season for travelling.'

Aboard a steamboat from Lyons (the roads were so bad they went by river), they had to negotiate bridges that were only six inches higher than the funnel of the boat. The smallest wave would have caused havoc.

'I would rather be in the open sea in a hurricane.'

Three months later they arrived in Rome. They were deeply distressed by the condition of the Jews there. 'I am informed,' observed Sir Moses, 'there are 3,500 Jews here, two-thirds of them poor. Four times a year 200 are obliged to attend a sermon preached in church for their conversion.' They were also prevented from trading or following their professions outside the ghetto.

While in Rome the Montefiores purchased silk damask richly embroidered in gold and silver for hangings for their Synagogue—the Holy Ark and pulpit. The Montefiores met in Rome Dr. Loewe and they spoke of their intended pilgrimage to Jerusalem, and invited him to accompany them. While there they received disastrous news of impending war between the Pasha of Egypt and the Sultan. Sir Moses was advised to return to London, but he could not be deterred.

On their voyage to Malta they enjoyed reading Psalms together and Lady Montefiore studied Arabic with Dr. Loewe. In Malta they dined at the Palace with the Governor and heard further alarming news. The plague was rife in Jerusalem. Nearly 50 people were dying daily. Sir Moses decided to proceed alone, but this was resisted by his wife:

'the expressions of Ruth furnished my heart at the moment with the language it most desired to use. "Entreat me not to leave thee, or to return from following after thee; for whither thou goest I will go, and where thou lodgest I will lodge!"'

They travelled together. A steam vessel, the *Megara*, took them to Alexandria, where the signs of war-preparations were on the quayside—a thousand of the Pasha's troops, most of them under fifteen years old!

In Beirut they equipped themselves with tents, horses and mules and set out through the mountains of Lebanon towards Safed, one of the four holy cities in the land of Israel. The Montefiores rode across the sandy plain by donkey and horse. Sir Moses was aware of the dangers:

'Our visit is not the most timely for our comfort, pleasure or safety; the political state of the country is most unsatisfactory and uncertain; a single day may bring about a complete change in the government of Syria and Palestine.'

He was soon proved right. While resting in tents near Sidon, their messenger was attacked. Dr. Loewe spent the night on guard with loaded pistols, the Montefiores keeping pistols at the ready as well.

Dr. Loewe.

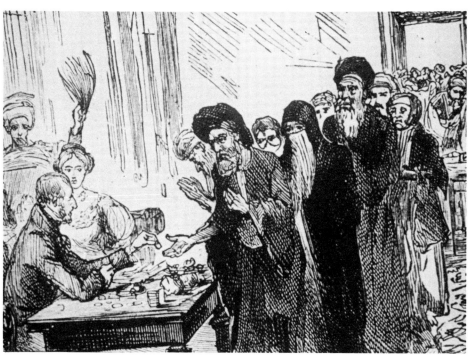

Sir Moses and Lady Montefiore distributing alms in Safed, 1839.

Census form of the Jews in Palestine 1839.

After a four hours' ride they reached Safed, on 21 May. The arrival was timely. The Jewish community had suffered during the revolt of the fellaheen in 1834, the earthquake of 1837 (in which 2,000 Jews in Safed had died), and the attack by Druze in 1838. Ten thousand Jews now lived in the four Holy Cities of Safed, Tiberias, Jerusalem and Hebron, largely on the charity of their brethren abroad. In Safed, the whole afternoon of 22 May was spent by Sir Moses and his wife seeing people, listening to their complaints and sorrows, and obtaining information respecting the cultivation of the land. To augment his information he engaged Dr. Loewe to undertake a census.

'It is a land that would produce almost everything in abundance, with very little skill and labour. I am sure if the plan I have in contemplation should succeed, it will be the means of introducing happiness and plenty into the Holy Land. In the first instance I shall apply to Mehemet Ali for a grant of land for 50 years for 100 or 200 villages. This grant obtained, I shall please heaven on my return to England to form a company for the cultivation of the land and the encouragement of our brethren in Europe to return to Palestine. The poverty of Jews in Safed is greater than anything that can be imagined in Europe. Many are starving. Great numbers died last year of hunger. I have found all anxious to be employed in agriculture. Many Jews now emigrate to New South Wales, Canada etc., but in the Holy Land they would find a greater certainty of success; here they will find wells, olives and vines and a land so rich as to require little manure. By degrees I hope to induce the return of thousands of our brethren to the Land of Israel.'

Having distributed money for the relief of earthquake sufferers, alms to the poor, and donations to schools and colleges, he explored the tomb of Hillel ('One of the most interesting sights I have ever seen in the Holy Land'). They then rode on a two-day journey to Tiberias, the route to which confirmed his plans:

'We rode through a beautiful country, a very long descent, winding round hills covered with olives, figs and pomegranates. In the plain we saw the richest land imaginable, though but a very small part of it was under cultivation.'

A tremendous reception greeted them in Tiberias. The local Governor had proclaimed a day's holiday in honour of this visit. The streets were crowded, people carried large torches and the whole town was illuminated. The Governor hoped Sir Moses would settle in the Holy Land and become a leader of his community, but what ensued were discussions on land cultivation with local Jewish representatives. On the ride from Tiberias to Eyn Louba, he observed more fertile land, sown with wheat, barley and oats, in need of efficient cultivation. From Djouni, they rode through more cultivated land:

'I have never seen any country so rich and beautiful. We rested under a grove of fig trees, in a garden surrounded by the most magnificent scenery; the spot might well have been termed a "garden of Eden", a very Paradise.'

Entering Jerusalem.

Jerusalem in 1839 was not like this. On their journey they met families fleeing from the city to escape the plague. Lady Montefiore set the scene:

'As we drew nearer to Jerusalem, the aspect of the surrounding country became more and more sterile and gloomy. The land was covered with thorns and briars (and) the melancholy desolateness of the rocky hills and valleys.'

Sir Moses exclaimed:

'Most fervently do I pray that the wilderness of Zion may again be like Eden, and her desert like the garden of the Lord.'

They had to pitch their tents on the Mount of Olives in quarantine, and when they entered Jerusalem they had to have guards to distance people in order to lessen the threat of contagion. Sir Moses assessed, with the Jewish community, the need to find work for the poor, particularly in agriculture.

For the Montefiores there was a special experience, as they rode through the valley of Jehoshaphat to the tomb of David. Europeans were forbidden to enter the tomb, but the Governor obtained permission for them. They toured the cave of Jeremiah and the tombs of the Kings, and Sir Moses was given a beautiful white Arabian horse to ride into Jerusalem, in recognition of his status and his personal friendship with Mehemet Ali. Riding towards Bethlehem Lady Montefiore noticed Rachel's Tomb needed repairing, so ordered an estimate for its restoration and had an entrance chamber added to it. The Governor of Hebron offered them the presidency of Jewish charities and schools. They visited the Cave of Machpelah and the Mosque, but they had to make a hurried exit from the Mosque when Moslems began attacking Jews who were joining the travellers. After that Sir Moses had twenty mounted and armed guards sent from Jerusalem and gave the Governor of Jerusalem a telescope in gratitude. Instructing Dr. Loewe to take the census of the Jewish population was not easy in a land where it was believed the plague had struck because King David had carried out a census.

There *was* plague in Jaffa, Sir Moses' next destination, so they rode on to Haifa. In quarantine outside the town, they heard that Jews from Safed had fled because of attacks by Druze. No security from plunder existed in Palestine, yet rumours about roads infested with robbers did not deter Sir Moses in his decision to take the road to Beirut, neither did the rugged mountain pass and the precipices. On the road, at Bassatin, they met three men of the Metouáli tribe who refused to give the party water. They were forced to hand over their jars and when returned they smashed the jars to pieces. Sir Moses discovered that their religion forbade them using objects which had been touched by people of a different creed. It was a poignant incident.

Sir Moses went to Alexandria with specific proposals:

'I am now anxious to have an interview with the Pasha at Alexandria, for the purpose of claiming security for the persons and property of the Jews in Palestine, and particularly for those at Safed and Tiberias, where they are continually exposed to insult, robbery and murder.'

Other requests included having the walls of Tiberias repaired, allowing Jews to give evidence in court cases, land and villages to be rented on a 50-year lease, provision for Sir Moses to send people to assist the cultivation of the land, and a decree to open banks in Beirut, Jaffa, Jerusalem and Cairo. He was introduced to Boghoz Bey, the Minister of Finance, who forwarded the requests to Mehemet Ali. The next day Sir Moses in full uniform and Sheriff's chain went to the Pasha's Palace. He had met the Pasha in Cairo in 1827 but the latter stated he possessed no land in Palestine. He acknowledged the requests, but establishment of colonies, agricultural changes, religious toleration and justice took second place to the proposed banks.

Professor Yehoshua Ben-Arieh comments on this 1839 visit in 'The Rediscovery of the Holy Land in the Nineteenth Century':

'The real awakening to the idea of Jewish agricultural settlement came with Montefiore's visit. Encouraged by this enthusiasm, Montefiore drew up a scheme for leasing two hundred villages in Galilee for settlement by Jewish farmers. Before submitting the plan to Mehemet Ali he discussed it with the British consul in Jerusalem, who, while advising caution, nevertheless agreed that a move to agriculture would improve the position of the Jews. Mehemet Ali, suspecting that the plan might lead to some sort of independence for the Jews, procrastinated while hinting that it did not seem feasible. Events decided the matter: the Egyptians were forced to leave and negotiations ended. Montefiore pursued his efforts on behalf of the Jews of Palestine in other ways.'

From Alexandria, the voyage to Malta was marred by a *three-week* stay in the heat in the quarantine harbour there. They did not reach Dover until 5 September. Almost immediately, Sir Moses departed on the Damascus Mission. When he returned, projects for the Holy Land had to be postponed. Mehemet Ali had ceased to be the ruler of Syria, since the Egyptians had been driven out of Syria and Palestine by Ottoman forces. Had war not occurred between Egypt and Turkey, whole villages might have been inhabited by Jewish agriculturists and Sir Moses' view of progress and emancipation endorsed in the 1840s.

This was the message of Colonel Charles Churchill to whom Sir Moses had given the Sultan's firman to deliver to the Jewish community in Damascus. In a remarkable letter to Sir Moses from Damascus, dated 14 June 1841, Churchill presented his suggestions:

'My most anxious desire (is) to see your countrymen endeavour once more to resume their existence as a people. But two things are indispensably necessary. Firstly that the Jews will themselves take up the matter universally *and* unanimously. *Secondly that the European powers will aid them in their views. It is for the Jews to make a commencement. Let them meet, concert and petition. In fact, the agitation must be simultaneous throughout Europe. The result would be that you would conjure up a new element in Eastern Diplomacy. Were the resources which you possess steadily directed towards the regeneration of Syria and Palestine there cannot be a doubt, but that, under the blessing of the most High, those Countries would amply repay the undertaking, and that you would end by obtaining the sovereignty of at least Palestine. These countries* must *be rescued from the group of ignorant and fanatical rulers, that the march of civilisation* must *progress and that its various elements of commercial prosperity* must *be developed. Syria and Palestine in a word must be taken under European protection, governed in the sense and according to the spirit of European Administration. It is for the Jews to be* ready, *against such a crisis in diplomacy. It could only be as subjects of the Porte that you could commence to regain a footing in Palestine. In all enterprizes, men must be prepared to make great sacrifices, whether of time, health, or resources. To reflect calmly before commencing an undertaking, and once begun, to carry it through, vanquishing, surmounting, triumphing over every obstacle. This is worthy of man's existence, and carries with it, its own reward, if the judgement is sound, the head clear and the heart honest. I will keep you 'au fait' of all that passes in this Country if you wish it.'*

In a second letter to Sir Moses on 15 August 1842, Colonel Churchill made a more explicit proposal:

'Direct your most strenuous attention towards the land of your Fathers with the view of doing all in your power to ameliorate the condition of your brethren now residing

there. My proposition is that the Jews in England conjointly with their brethren on the continent of Europe should make an application to the British Government through the Earl of Aberdeen to accredit and send out a fit and proper person to reside in Syria for the sole and express purpose of superintending and watching over the interests of the Jews residing in that Country, an acknowledged agent for the Jewish people resident in Syria and Palestine under the auspices and sanction of Great Britain.'

The Board of Deputies considered this on 8 November and resolved that it was precluded from originating any measures for carrying out the benevolent views of Colonel Churchill regarding the Jews of Syria, but it would contribute to any measures emanating from the general body of the Jews throughout Europe. The matter was considered to be of great importance but was deferred for further deliberation.

After Sir Moses' second visit to Palestine, intensive correspondence was initiated between the communities, Talmudic academies, welfare institutions and himself. In 1842 he sent a printing press to Israel Drucker in Jerusalem and in 1843 at his own expense a qualified physician with a well-stocked dispensary to attend the Jewish sick in Jerusalem. This followed reports of the epidemic diseases, malaria, cholera, typhoid, smallpox and dysentery.

Another outbreak of cholera and the activities of Christian missionaries impelled the third visit in 1848. Europe was the setting for revolutionary upheavals but Sir Moses and Lady Montefiore were in Beirut, ominously being shown the graves of unfortunate travellers who had died while in quarantine. As in 1839, they visited Safed, Tiberias, Jerusalem and Hebron. In Nazareth they experienced the old blood libel calumny, when a woman accused them of stealing her child. Fortunately the child was found but the incident reminded them of the potency of superstitions. In Jerusalem they distributed £5,000 to aid the relief of cholera victims' families and the poor, and Sir Moses founded a small textile plant. Lady Montefiore had remarked of the poor in Jerusalem: 'Energy and talent exist. Nothing is needed but protection and encouragement.' The 1848 visit had been a brief one to succour the community in a time of desperation.

The Jewish Hospital, Jerusalem, 1855.

For the next seven years Jerusalem was never far from their thoughts. Sir Moses promoted the city at the Great Exhibition of 1851, displaying two vases by Mordechai Schnitzler of Jerusalem, and spent hundreds of pounds on plans drawn up by architects and on consultations with medical authorities for a proposed hospital in the city. In 1853, the Rev. S. M. Isaacs of the North American Relief Society asked him to forward £145 annually to help poor Jews in Jerusalem and told him the Juda Touro legacy of 50,000 dollars was to be used for the same purpose, and entrusted to Sir Moses. He advised Gershon Kursheedt, one of the executors of the legacy, that the money should be used to build a hospital. Later a new hospital was erected by the Rothschilds.

Despite discouragements from Western scepticism and Eastern lethargy Sir Moses was now unremittingly engaged in creating better conditions for Jews in Palestine. There were, by the 1850s, Jewish majorities in Jerusalem, Tiberias and Safed, and yet some of these poor had sold their children to monasteries to spare them from starvation. An Appeal Fund realised £19,887 from Western Jewish communities, but the poverty remained. Sir Moses explained the situation to the Chief Rabbi in England, the Rev. Dr. N. M. Adler:

'Poverty in the East differs vastly from the like calamity experienced in Western Europe, inasmuch as the capability to relieve is in the East confined within the narrowest bounds, and restricted to a very limited number.'

In August 1854 the trustees of the Appeal Fund on behalf of Jews in the Holy Land published their first report. It earmarked funds for relieving distress and promoting industry and recorded that the Montefiores would go to the Holy Land to inspect and examine the charities and begin new foundations of land cultivation.

This fourth visit was crucial. A fresh crisis had broken out in Palestine with cholera and famine. The communities' funds from Poland had dried up because of the Crimean War, which also led to rising food prices. The Montefiores left England on 13 May 1855 accompanied by Mr. Kursheedt, Dr. Loewe and the Guedallas, his nephew and niece. They took a different route, resting in Prague, where they visited the ancient synagogue and received numerous deputations from communal, educational and literary institutions. In Constantinople, they met Lord Stratford de Redcliffe, Ali Pasha and Rechid Pasha and then the Sultan at the Palace. The latter praised Sir Moses' philanthropy and humanity, conferred on him the order of Medjidjeh, and gave him a new decree permitting him to purchase land (normally forbidden to non-Ottoman subjects).

A Takht Trivan (sedan chair), similar to the one used by the Montefiores.

74

We were fortunate to find Sir Moses' hand-written notebook of his visit to the Holy Land in 1855, published now for the first time. He records

'Laus Deo. Jaffa. Thursday 19th July, 1855.

I contrived to rise at 6 and attended prayers. A deputation of about 12 Hahamim—the heads of the several congregations, arrived from Jerusalem with an address from each Congregation and to accompany us to the Holy City. Achmet Aga sent his head officer with five soldiers and horses for my dear Jud and I to take us to Jerusalem. Finzi of Acre arrived with his Takht Trivan. The Governor of Jaffa sent his officer to say he had appointed him with ten soldiers to guard us to Jerusalem, but I made my thanks and declined the honour, there being so many persons with us. Mr. Kayat and his brother were with us for a long time. Mr. Dixon and they strongly recommend the cultivation of the land, the raising of silk engaging the people with the cocoons, a mill for pressing the oil from seed and a skane flour mill. We started ¼ to 5. My dear Jud in her Takht Trivan, myself in another. We were accompanied by the Governor of Jaffa, the Caidi, ten soldiers and one officer from Jaffa, six soldiers and one officer who came from Jerusalem to conduct us there, also all the Jerusalem deputation, with our own mules, camels and horses and a multitude of people. We reached Ramleh ¼ past 8. At Ramleh the Governor and the English Consul paid us a visit, having met us on the way to offer us their houses. The Consul insists on going with us to Jerusalem.'

'Laus Deo. Friday 20th July. Under the Walls of Jerusalem, near the Jaffa Gate.

Last night we had but three hours' sleep and started before two o'clock in the morning. We reached Abou Ghosh soon after 8 where we found a tent pitched for us. We rested an hour. When in sight of Jerusalem, Mr. and Mrs. Finn, British Consul, the Haham Bashi David Abulafi and all the Hahamim they rode with us to our tent. But I never suffered so much fatigue, and I may add fright in any journey in my life. The roads were truly terrific and God only knows how we reached the end of our journey in safety. Accept, oh merciful God of Israel, my humble and warmest thanks for bringing my dear wife and myself once again to the Gates of thy Holy City, the City of Zion.'

'Laus Deo. Saturday.

Very fatigued and weak.'

'Laus Deo. Sunday 22nd July.

Achmet Aga came from Nablus, travelled all night to see us.'

'Laus Deo. Monday 23rd July, 1855. Outside the walls of Jerusalem.

Mr. Rogers, the B.C. of Haifa, came from Mr. Finn to say it would be requisite to present the letters and Firman to the Governor today, as the Governor was going with the troops to Hebron. As soon as poles could be procured for my chair I was carried into Jerusalem by the Jaffa Gate. We were received with distinction, pipes, coffee, etc. I gave the Governor the letter which His Highness, Rechid Pasha, gave me for him, also that (from) the Governor at Beirut and the official letters I had brought from Constantinople. The first one was respecting the hospital, then that regarding cultivation of the land. I asked him for a piece of ground for the hospital, either within or without the city. He promised he would go himself and look out for the best place. The Governor then sent to summon a Council. In less than an hour the Council assembled, seven old men; all the papers were read over with great formality to them all standing while the Firman was being read. The Council expressed the same willingness as the Governor to meet my desire in every way possible, and would look for a spot for the hospital. I asked for a large space that there might be a good garden. The Commander of the Garrison then took us to his rooms and treated us with pipes, coffee and sherbet.'

Sir Moses' presence in Jerusalem was interpreted by poor Jews as the panacea, as though he had the power to relieve all sufferings and deprivations. However, he envisaged his rôle as the initiator of practical, lasting projects for self-sufficiency, and invited representatives of the Holy Cities to provide statistics on their institutions and requirements. Skilled agriculturists were also included, to discuss the practicability of commencing new land schemes. Sir Moses' plans were appropriate and timely:

'The Patriarch of a Greek Convent paid us a long visit in our tents. He said the place was fast becoming a European city. He had been 47 years in Jerusalem. The first 20 years only one or two strangers arrived, afterwards they increased gradually to five or seven, then 10 or 15, and now most numerous. The cultivators of the land have now rather more protection, and agricultural permits have better prospect of success.'

In his 1855 diary, Sir Moses recalls the events after his first visit to the Governor on 23 July:

'Laus Deo. Monday 23rd July, 1855. Outside the Walls of Jerusalem.

As soon as poles could be procured for my chair I was carried into Jerusalem by the Jaffa Gate. I went to Mr. Finn's then he and his attachés accompanied me to the Governor. I was carried to the Western Wall, and prayed for the health and happiness of my dear wife, my brothers and sisters and their children. I then went to the Synagogue, it was very full. Minhar. After prayers were read, returned immediately to our tents, dreadfully fatigued, but most thankful. We dined and took our fast. We had Minyhan in our tent, when the evenings prayers and lamentations were read till 9 o'clock.

Laus Deo. Tuesday 24th July.

A dreadfully hot day, the wind filled the tents with sand and dust, almost blinded us. We had Minyhan in our tents and read the prayers and lamentations in the morning. Afterwards I read the Lamentations of Jeremiah and part of the Book of Job. 5, Minha. 7, Evening prayers. 20 minutes to 8, broke our fast. Very weak and fatigued. Achmet Aga, his son and grandson partook of our repast. He brought his Jester and a lad that sang well. As Achmet's son is to leave for Hebron in command of 50 horses I gave him a revolver.

Laus Deo. Wednesday 25th July. Opposite the Walls, in the Tent.

At 9 the Governor with a number of attendants paid us a visit. He gave me the Firman for the Synagogue (rebuilding an old one), also copies of the Turkish letters I brought from Constantinople for the Hospital and cultivation of the lands. His Excellency said that he was desirous to do everything that I desired, and that I would consider him my son. If I should go to Hebron after next week he would accompany me himself, and tomorrow we are to see the Mosque of Omar. I recommend the son of Achmet to him, and he promised to give him the command of 100 horses. Mr. Finn paid us a visit, I

The 'Hurva' Synagogue.

A very early photograph of the Mosque of Omar.

delivered into his hands the Firman the Governor gave me for the rebuilding of the Synagogue.'

'Laus Deo. 26th July.

Early this morning we all went to the Seraglio and met the Governor at 8 o'clock. He gave us pipes and coffee and in a few moments he preceded us to the Mosque of Omar. Every person but ourselves had been excluded, and guards placed outside the gates, and 100 soldiers with their officers within.

Laus Deo. Friday 27th July, 1855. Opposite Walls. In the Tent.

The Sheik of the Mosque of the family in whose care it has been for above 770 years brought for my dear Jud and myself and Dr. L. some pieces of stone from the most holy part of the Mosque. Before 10 my dear Jud and I and Dr. L. went into the city to the house where the weaving is taught. Repast and prepared for Sabbath. About ½ past five the Governor with his Interpreter and some officers. He came to take leave of us, as he was going to Hebron to settle the troubles of that place. He was extremely polite, he said he had given directions to his Council to comply with all my requests and kindly said he put the city at my disposal.'

What Sir Moses was endeavouring to achieve in the city emerges from his diary entries for 31 July and 1 August:

'Laus Deo. Tuesday 31st July.

The day has been dreadfully hot. 10, my dear Jud, Dr. L. and myself paid the Haham Bashi a visit. Literally surrounded by about 20 Hahamim. He wishes me to buy them houses and land that they may pay their debts, and he consented to send his young daughter to a school if my dear Jud established one for teaching Hebrew and sewing. We afterwards went to see a piece of ground belonging to Mr. Perez near Wall of the City, two furlongs, but very near the place that cattle is slaughtered, which is a terrible nuisance in the Jewish quarter.

Laus Deo. Wednesday 1st August.

No one can possibly express the vexation I feel here. Achmet Aga sent an excuse. He could not go to measure the land, he must first send to Ali Aga for his consent to sell it. This is all an excuse. Have patience. The Haham Bashi didn't give the notice this morning at the Synagogue regarding the Girls' school. I said to him if it was not done this afternoon I would have nothing more to do with the Sephardim Congregation. Half past 9. Was carried in the City to the Weaver's house. The Agricultural Committee of Safed met me, when the Sephardim members said they did not understand yesterday. I dismissed them

*and placed three Ashkenasim on the Committee in their stead, and settled to engage 35
families at Safed and 13 at Bokea.'*

A committee of practical agriculturists was appointed for Safed to select land,
and he provided the 35 families with the means to begin agricultural pursuits
and the promise of protection by local Governors. This likewise applied to
Bokea, and 30 families were funded in Tiberias, with an instructor to supervise
the establishment.

The search was to find and buy land to the west of the Holy City, adjoining
the high road from Jerusalem to Hebron, so that the Jewish community could
work the land and build the boundary wall. Achmet Agha Dizdar, ex-Governor
of Jerusalem, owned land for sale, selling land in Jerusalem to a non-Moslem
foreigner creating a precedent.

'Laus Deo. Thursday 2nd August.

*Went at half past nine with Dr. Loewe, Mr. Kursheedt and Dr. Frankel to Achmet
Aga's ground. We met the Achmet Aga and Haim Theresby. Dr. Loewe with the
assistance of several men took the measure of the ground belonging to Achmet Aga. It was
4 o'clock before he finished. Achmet Aga asks 120,000 ps. (£1000) for his ground. So
much for friendly professions.*

Laus Deo. Friday 3rd August.

*I was too weak to go to the city today. I could neither write nor read . . . I was unable to
do anything myself today. Half past five dear Jud prepared for Sabbath. At 6 Dr. L.
returned. He found great difficulty in getting any house for the school, as he was asked 4
times its value. The lowest was 21,000 piasters for three years, to be paid in advance.
Achmet Aga would not take a piaster less than 120,000.*

Laus Deo. Saturday 4th August. Jerusalem. Opposite the Walls. In the tent.

*Prayers in the tent, with Minyhan. The day was dreadfully hot. Received a great number
of visitors, both male and female. The evening cool, wind high and fresh. I was very
weak. Achmet Aga came about 9, evening, and I left him with Dr. L. and gave the Dr.
full powers to conclude the purchase of the land. I went to bed about 10. Dr. said the
business was settled at the original price asked.'*

Sir Moses was surprised by the price he had to pay for the land, as he had noted
in his diary entry for 2 August. This was because Achmet Agha Dizdar had
been a friend since 1839 and, according to Dr. Loewe, had replied to Sir
Moses' inquiry about the purchase of the land with this panegyric:

*'You are my friend, my brother, the apple of my eye, take possession of it at once. This
land I hold as an heirloom from my ancestors. I would not sell it to any person for
thousands of pounds, but to you I give it without any money: it is yours, take possession
of it.'*

Dr. Loewe, acting as Sir Moses' amanuensis and interpreter, stated that the
following day Achmet Agha Dizdar had a more realistic business proposition:

*'You are my friend, my brother; by my beard, my head, I declare this is the case. Tell Sir
Moses to give me a souvenir of one thousand pounds sterling.'*

The purchase was confirmed in the hall of justice and the contract of sale read
aloud: 'By permission of the Sublime Porte and the Imperial Throne, may the
Lord of Creation preserve them, and in conformity with the letters on that
subject from the Grand Vizier to Sir Moses Montefiore (Baronet), the pride of
the people of Moses, the man of prudence, the son of Joseph Eliyahu, Sir
Moses purchases a piece of land for the purpose of establishing thereon a
hospital for the poor of the Israelites who reside in Jerusalem, and does with it
as he pleases.'

'Laus Deo. Sunday 5th August.

Went to the Weaver's at ½ past 9. Went to see the schoolhouse. The Greek monk of the convent in Jerusalem came to see me. I said we had paid them a very high price for the house we have taken for the weavers, £50, but he said it had cost building £3,500. Complained that the Turks took so much money from them.' (Sir Moses had founded a vocational training school and workshop to teach young Jews the art of weaving. He had arranged for three of them to go to Preston to learn the trade, and on this visit scrutinised the progress at the house where the weaving was taught.) *'We have paid a deposit to Achmet Aga for his land. I have purchased it for £1,000. Dr. Loewe also concluded the rent for three years for the schoolhouse at 18,000 ps. (between £50 and £60) to be paid in advance according to the custom of the country. The house is in the very best street in the Jewish quarter, a large house with many rooms and a garden. Standing and very airy. Offered to the Hahaim Levi of Jaffa 40,000 piasters for his ground at Jaffa. I remained with the Committee from Tiberias from ½ past 9, when, worn down with fatigue, I returned to our tents. This climate is very fine mornings and evenings cool, but the sun dreadfully hot.*

Above. *The lament of the faithful at the wailing wall Jerusalem. Bauernfeind. (The Royal Academy).*

Right. *Pilgrims and the Takht Trivan at the Damascus gate.*

Laus Deo. Friday 10th August.
Drew at 10/ds. sight on NMR & Co. £150, order of Jusef Mascheoff. Returned the visit of the Greek and Armenian Patriarchs. Their hospitality was truly kind. And going, I gave to each £10 for the poor. Paid Achmet Aga for the land and the expenses outstanding with Mascheoff, and amount owing to the expenses of the Weaver's house. Drew on Messrs. N.M.R. & Sons, dated 8th August 1855, £200 at 10 days' sight, to the order of Messrs. Jacob Valero.
Laus Deo. Sunday 12th August.
My dear Jud and I went in our Takht Trivan to the land we had purchased, and all the company met us there. We were so pleased with the situation as to order immediately the removal of our tents to this place. At 5 said prayers with Minyhan, on the land. We had many visits, Achmet Aga etc. A lovely starlight night.
Laus Deo. Monday 13th August. On the land, Jerusalem.
The Bankers came and I drew £70 and £430 on Messrs. N.M.R. and Sons at 10 days' sight, to the order of Jusef Mascheoff. This with £100 or £200 more I shall distribute to the poor here. While we were at breakfast under the olive trees a Mussulman school of about 50 boys came to congratulate us on taking possession of the ground and sang a hymn. A second school came with more than 50 boys. We received a letter from Joseph Sebag, dated 30th July, our friend Baron Solomon Rothschild has departed this life, to my sincere regret. My dear Jud and myself received from him and his dear excellent wife the kindest marks of friendship.
Laus Deo. Wednesday 15th August.
I went in a Takht Trivan to the city at 11 to witness the opening of the Girls' School. My dear Jud rode there. Mr. Kursheedt and Mr. and Mrs. Guedalla were present. There were also about 80 children of the Sephardim, but no child of the Ashkenasim.

79

About 11 o'clock, Dr. Loewe read some Psalms and then addressed the children in Hebrew, afterwards in Spanish—a most admirable and affecting address.' (This girls' school offered instruction in the pursuits of needlework, dressmaking, embroidery and domestic occupations.) *'I went back to our ground, and with God's blessing assisted in laying the first stone of the hospital. Dr. Loewe read the inscription that was deposited there, read some prayers and we sang some Psalms.'* (Sir Moses also recommended siting a windmill nearby, to provide cheap flour for the poor.)

'Laus Deo. Thursday 16th August. On our ground. Jerusalem.

Early this morning the Haham Bashi with the 9 Hahamim of Mr. Guedalla's Midrash paid us a long visit. I read the general congratulations of them on the purchase of the land and laying down the stone of the Hospital, likewise of the schools. My dear Jud found herself very poorly this afternoon. She had intended to have taken a ride to see the Western Wall and to call on Mordecai Schnitzler, but she was compelled to go to bed at 5. I sent for Dr. Frankel, he came and recommended quietness.'

'Laus Deo. Friday 17th August. Tent.

The Secretary of the Pasha with the Edam Bey, the Acting Governor with the Governor of Jaffa came to see me about 8 this morning, to acquaint me that Kemal Pasha gave his hearty consent to my purchase at Jaffa. My dear Jud passed a restless night. Dr. Frankel saw her at five this morning, she has a slight attack of diarrhoea. The heat has been dreadfully oppressive.'

'Laus Deo. Sunday 19th August.

Thanks to God, Jud is without fever though very weak. At ½ past 8 this morning 21 guns were fired from the Castle, it being the anniversary of the Emperor of Austria. The scribe brought up the declaration title for the purchase of the Jaffa ground, but it was not drawn up in the words I agreed to at the Consul. He is to alter it and have the Cadis Seal affixed to it today. I felt extremely fatigued today and was obliged to go into my tent at 9.'

'Laus Deo. Monday 20th August. Think and Thank.

My dear Jud improving. Much plagued with the people committee from Hebron. In distributing the money sent to them the Portuguese give to all a share, rich and poor. The Germans only give to the poor.'

Apart from exhaustion from the heat and haggling over land prices, Sir Moses experienced only one incident to mar this constructive and fruitful time in Jerusalem. It had occurred on 6 August:

'Whilst at prayers this morning we were disturbed by the voices of many hundred persons, men, women and children, who came saying they were starving, and the men wanted work. One man, a Russian from Moscow, encouraged the others to violence, but Dr. Loewe persuaded him to go with some of our people to our place of cooking, and directed he should have bread and coffee given to him. Dr. Loewe continued for some hours taking down the names and hearing the troubles they complained of, but about 2 o'clock the Russian insisted on having meat and again became most outrageous in his conduct, when I ordered him to be taken to the British Consul. It required a dozen of our guards to take him there. He fought like a tiger and was dragged there. The Consul ordered him to be confined.'

On Sir Moses' advice, the Governor had the public slaughterhouses removed from the Jewish quarter to a place outside the city walls, and although Sir Moses gave funds to distribute among the poor, he argued that the future depended upon the institutions created for agriculture and industry, not charity. The Montefiores left Jerusalem, having initiated numerous projects. Less than two years later they would return to inspect the progress made.

'Laus Deo. Tuesday 21st August.

We rose at 5 but were detained till 9 for mules. The Deputy Governor came to our tents at

Tiberias · מבריא · Тиверіа

Zion · ציון · Сіонъ

Saffed · צפת · Сафеда

All the pictures on this page and the next come from a beautiful little book bound in inlaid olive wood. Opposite each picture is a group of dried wild flowers which have been grown in the neighbourhood shown—probably a souvenir of their first visit.

Jerusalem · ירושלם · Іерусалима

Hebron   חברון   Хеврона

קבר רחל

Grabe Rahel's   гробницы Рахили

8 to see us safely start; he immediately gave orders for the muleteer with whom I had made an engagement to furnish 9 horses and 24 mules, and they all soon bestirred themselves. Our guards were in attendance, hundreds of Jews were on the ground. When fairly off we had a pleasant ride to Rachel's tomb which we entered and read prayers, gave some money to the poor and then mounted our Takht Trivan and reached the Pools of Solomon at 12. We had a very numerous company of Jews, Achmet Aga, etc. We had some of the finest water possible from the springs. We found the air fresh and pleasant. At 3 we set off again, and thanks to God, reached Hebron about ½ past 7. Two hours before a huge deputation of Jews met us to accompany us into the City and half an hour before we entered our encampment a Guard of Honour sent by the Pasha met us and conducted us with music to our tents. We were very fatigued, particularly my dear Jud, whose Takht Trivan met with an accident. It fell and gave her great alarm, but by God's mercy she was not hurt, only frightened. The Heads of the Congregation had prepared for us a most capital dinner but my dear Jud and myself were but too happy to get to bed the moment our tent was erected. We took a little soup in bed and that was all, but our party said the fowls and beef were excellent.'

'Laus Deo. Wednesday 22nd August. Hebron. In our old field.

Said our prayers, with Minyan. The morning was delightfully cold. Poor Jud and myself are suffering today by the fatigue of yesterday. The Pasha Kamil came in his state uniform with the Governor of Hebron, also Mr. Gilbert, the Governor of Jerusalem's Secretary and paid us a long visit. Deputations from the Jews also came and the ladies of Hebron. At 4 I went in my Takht Trivan to the Camp to return the Kamil's visit. This day being the 8 Elul, the anniversary of the happy release of our poor innocent co-religionists at Damascus, I gave a treat to the muleteers and all our attendants. We had two sheep killed for them, with plenty of vegetables and bread. We had an immense bonfire, Turkish music, and a set of men who amused the party with jumping, singing and fencing. There were many hundreds of lookers-on, both Jews and Mussulmen. The Jews sang Psalms, we gave them wine and cake. About 10 my dear Jud and I withdrew into our tent, but the entertainment continued till midnight. The price asked for the piece of ground was £50, but I didn't know it before I went to bed. I sent the Governor of Jerusalem for his soldiers this evening 12 sheep, and ordered 12 more to be sent him early tomorrow morning.

Laus Deo. 23rd August, 1855. Tents of Hebron.

This morning on being prepared to complete the purchase of the piece of ground, I desired Dr. Loewe to see the parties and offer them £30 for it, but they said they had considered the matter and must have 50,000 piasters for it. Of course there was an end of the matter. I went and returned the visit of the present Governor of Jaffa. He was anxious I should accept from him a present of a very beautiful horse which he had brought out of the stables for me to see, but I declined his kind offer. When I was in Synagogue today I gave the eldest of the Portuguese and German Congregations £300 for the Committee, being £130 for the Hahamim and Officers of their Synagogue, and £170 for the poor. Rabbi Moshe Khamhi of the Sephardim, an intelligent man, would make a good agent.'

'Laus Deo. Hebron. 24th August.

Glory to the Almighty in this Holy Land. My Blessed and Honoured Mother entered into Eternal Glory on the 10th Elul. (August 24th) Peace to her soul, the Glory of my head. I rose at 5, many came to see us off, the Haham Bashi and the Chief Rabbi with many Jews came to give us their blessings.

The first three hours of this day's journey, on leaving Hebron, was very mountainous and rocky, but afterwards extremely easy and pleasant. The weather continues very hot. My dear Jud's health has improved and she rode for an hour on horseback. We have a very large party, Ali Achmet with 30 soldiers and his little son, also Achmet Aga.'

'Laus Deo. Kiryatelpraye. Sunday August 26th.

We rose at 4, and at 5 m.40 we started and after an agreeable ride of 4 hours over very level plains we reached at ½ past 9 the house of the British Consul at Ramlah. Here we took some repose and took lunch at ½ past 12. Our host at Ramlah is the British Vice-Consular Agent but has no English Flag. He has two brothers as V.C. Agents to Prussia and America. They live all in that one house, all the latter have their flags flying here. We dined at 1. Finch brought the provisions, and dressed our dinner. Our host gave me some tobacco which grew on his own land. Dr. Loewe went with one of the brothers to see some land they wished to sell me. It is about one hour's distance from Ramlah. The three brothers' wives were introduced to us; the wife of the E.C. was only 20 years old, had 5 children since her marriage, three had died but the eldest was a fine lad between 9 and 10, the youngest only 15 days old. She was married at 11 years of age, her husband was 19. They are all Greek Christians and agreeable and gay women. The Governor of Ramlah and the Cadi came to pay us a visit and accompanied us some way out of the town. The weather has been excessively hot. Dr. Loewe went with a brother of the B.V. Consul to see some land he had to sell, about an hour's distance from Ramlah. We started at 6, and thanks to Almighty God, reached Jaffa safely at 9 a.15. Our Guards amused us a little, riding and firing their guns at each other.'

Sir Moses gave vent to his frustrations about climate and land deals:

'Laus Deo. Jaffa. Monday 27th August.

I feel the weather most trying at this place. The heat is dreadful. The East is, as far as my experience goes, a hard trial to patience. After a great number of hours and days passed at Jerusalem and the great expense incurred to complete my purchase of Rabbi Judah Levy's land at Jaffa, I find at the last moment, when I am here, pay the purchase money, and take possession of the land, that the person in possession claims to hold a lease of the property, and now refuses to give it up, although she declared to Dr. Loewe in the presence of Rabbi Levy her anxiety that I should purchase the property, and that she would leave the land, house etc. instantly, having purchased another place more suitable to her purpose. Mr. Kayat says the American Consul told him she claims 7,000 piasters for improvements before she will give me possession. I have sent Dr. L. to see her before I pay the purchase money. I shall take possession by placing a man there. Mr. Kayat wishes to sell me some land and a house for 10,000 piasters, or to borrow £1000 with c 10%. The French Consul of Jaffa, Mr. F. E. Philibert, a very intelligent and agreeable man, paid us a visit. The Dr. returned late but has, I hope, brought the parties to an understanding, which will lead to an amiable settlement tomorrow. I have been dreadfully plagued today with all kinds of visitors. I have settled with most of the men and muleteers. I am dreadfully cheated and imposed upon, but tho' I know it well, I am obliged to submit; everyone ordering and I only paying but, thank God, a few weeks will now bring it to an end.'

The next day brought a change in fortune:

'Laus Deo. Jaffa. Tuesday, 28th August.

I passed a restless night, the heat was intolerable. I had dreadful perspirations, my night linen quite wet. Today I was kept in suspense regarding the settlement of the land till an hour after the arrival of the steamboat, but blessed be God, at last at 2 the papers were signed and the money paid. I had deputed Mrs. Minor to conduct the work and to remain in charge of the property for three months, and gave her 50 sovereigns to defray the expenses. I have appointed Rabbi Judah Levy to act as the Ecclesiastical Governor, and to take care that no improper person was allowed to be on the estate. The British and American Consuls passed some hours with us. Mrs. Kayat and her sister paid us a visit, also the Governor, and I believe every officer in the town from the highest to the lowest. We had Minyhan here this morning. At ½ p. 3 my dear Jud, Jemima Guedalla and myself were conducted by the British Consul and Mr. Butler to the waterside, where we took leave of them and Dr. Frankel, Achmet Aga, Ali Aga and his son accompanied us to the ship. And now O merciful God of our Fathers, Abraham, Isaac and Jacob, conduct us in health and in peace to the desired end of our voyage. Send thine Angel with us that the sea and the wind may be calm, that health may be in the breeze, that peace and good feeling may be with us. May, O God of Israel, bless my dear wife with long life and happiness, and may my weak and feeble efforts for the support of our Holy Religion and the happiness of my brethren in the Holy Land be accepted for all my weakness and sins! Amen. We weighed anchor at ¼ to 6 and proceeded on our way with the blessing of the Almighty to Alexandria. The evening and night were mild and beautiful, a lovely moon. I took my berth on the deck.

Laus Deo. Wednesday 29th August. On board the Schild.

The early morning and sunrise magnificent and the weather all day lovely, a pleasant breeze and the air mild and agreeable.

Laus Deo. Thursday 30th August. Think and Thank. In the harbour of Alexandria. We entered the harbour about 6 this morning, having laid off the land from 12 last night till after sunrise this morning for a pilot. Mr. Roquerbi immediately came on board to offer us his services and left one of his servants to attend us during our stay at Alexandria.'

This 1855 visit had far-reaching implications. His practical and financial contributions laid the basis for the agricultural settlements of the 1880s, even if the inspiration for the latter came from the radical social movements in Eastern Europe. In 1855 self-reliance was his message for the Jewish communities, if they wished to overcome poverty and resist oppression. Back in England he arranged agreements with Holmans of Canterbury to erect the windmill for £1,450, corresponded with the institutions that he had created, and decided to return soon to supervise their progress. Having resigned from the Presidency of the British Board of Deputies again, he and Lady Montefiore, Kursheedt and Dr. Thomas Hodgkin were on their travels by February 1857. Dr. Hodgkin, the Quaker physician who treated poor Jews in the east end of London often without charge, had researched into carcinoma, diabetes and cholera and 'On Some Morbid Appearances of the Absorbent Glands and Spleen' (later named Hodgkin's disease). He travelled with Sir Moses to Italy in 1859 and Morocco in 1863–1864, and nursed Lady Montefiore during her final illness in 1862. In Malta, Sir Moses picked up ideas on rearing silkworms from the Governor, Sir William Reid, and proposed to introduce the experiment in the Holy Land. He also met Laurence Oliphant whose scheme for the settlement of Jews in Gilead played another part in the colonisation of Palestine.

By May, he was in Jaffa, delighted to see the numerous new houses constructed in the previous 22 months. Dizdar provided the Montefiores with

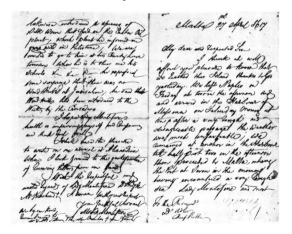

Letter written by Sir Moses from Malta.

five soldiers to accompany them in the Holy Land and offered more land for cultivation. In Jerusalem they had reports from the representatives of the various projects, and visited the dispensary, the girls' school and the weaving establishment. Sir Moses was reassured by the progress made in these, but while preparations for the windmill were advancing, the proposed hospital met opposition. The German congregation preferred alms-houses. The outcome was the new plan for a residential quarter.

The essence of Sir Moses' scheme was to build round a square, houses equally allotted to Ashkenazi and Sephardi communities. Each house would have a garden in order to grow the vine, olive trees and vegetables, and every house would have wrought-iron windows for security. A central feature was a water reservoir system and the cultivation of mulberry trees (for silk-worms and fruit). A model of his plan is shown in the permanent exhibition in the windmill which he had erected.

The historic value of his initiative was only partially recognised at the time. He was laying the cornerstone of the new city of Jerusalem. This was the first Jewish presence outside the walls of the old city. On the return journey he stayed in Alexandria in one of the Pasha's palaces, used the royal carriages and was treated to magnificent entertainments. He hoped that better relations would result with the local Jewish community. Another royal reception at the palace in Cairo was followed by a visit to the railway at Tuck, a ride through the desert for 40 miles, and a view of ten thousand workers laying the track.

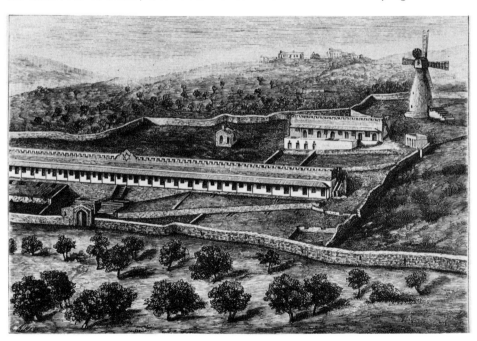

The Mishkenot Sha'ananim. The first Jewish quarter outside the walls of Jerusalem founded by Sir Moses in 1860.

Activities on behalf of the Holy Land continued. He reported to the Holy Land Committee his observations on the institutions created by the trustees, but there were setbacks. The weaving establishment and the girls' school closed in 1858 because they needed £300 per year to upkeep, and difficulties emerged over the building of the Juda Touro Almshouses. In June 1859 the local Governor suspended the project because the building was too near city fortifications. (The stone had been prepared, the foundations excavation and the doors, iron-work and windows sent out from England.) Eventually, in December, permission to continue was granted, but the delay had increased the cost dramatically, the builder having remained six months longer and workers retained pending a decision. The project continued and Sir Moses wished the inhabitants of the almshouses to be

'persons of excellent character, men well learned in our Law, who devote much of their time to study, and by whom a nice house, free of rent, in a pleasant situation, would be considered a boon.'

Sir Moses, the Chief Rabbi Dr. Adler, Mr. Kursheedt and Dr. Loewe named the almshouses 'Mishkenot Sha' ananim' (the dwellings of those who are at ease), to be shared equally by Ashkenazim and Sephardim:

'There are to be eight houses and a Synagogue for the Portuguese; a similar number of houses with a Synagogue for the German community; one house for the weaver and one for a Dispensary.'

There developed a conflict of interests between the Turkish authorities and Sir Moses' plans for Jerusalem. The Turks were keen to see a colony of Jews in Palestine but not poor Jews. If European Jews wished to return to the Holy Land and advance money to the Government, they would have land, liberty and protection. In contrast, Sir Moses sought from the Turkish Government further concessions for the expansion of institutions for indigent Jews. Progress had been made by 1862:

'a considerable number of almshouses and especially a large windmill are offering shelter, social advantages and employment to a great number of the poorer inhabitants.'

A sixth visit to the Holy Land began in 1863. He reached Constantinople, where the Sultan confirmed the concessions given to Sir Moses for the purchase of land and building of houses in Jerusalem. Ill-health prevented any further travel and Dr. Hodgkin persuaded him to return immediately to England.

By now support was flowing into the communities in Jerusalem, Hebron, Safed and Tiberias from West European Jewish communities and fund-raising had been placed on a sound organised footing. The economic conditions of local Jews in Palestine had gradually improved, aided by Sir Moses' continual concern for schools, synagogues, clinics and other welfare institutions.

In February 1865 Sir Moses was involved in meetings to renovate the water supply in Jerusalem. (Water was scarce in the summer. Most houses had no cisterns, so water had to be bought at exorbitant prices.) He discussed with Sir Henry James at the Ordnance Survey Office, Southampton, the survey of Jerusalem by British engineers and £100 was forwarded by the Syrian Improvement Fund Committee to the engineers towards expenses of excavations to provide an efficient water supply. In August, tragic news arrived. Sixty people a day were dying of cholera in Jerusalem. Fifteen per cent of the total population died that year. Unhealthy dwellings, poor water supply and poverty exacerbated the tragedy:

'No rain had fallen for many months, the harvest was spoilt, locusts covered the ground for miles around, the cholera had broken out in all its fury, famine and plague reigned supreme in the Holy Cities. In Jaffa, the corpses of the dead lay in the streets unburied. The once bustling seaport town was stricken with terror and awed into silence. All the towns and villages between Jaffa and Jerusalem were affected. The gates of the latter were closed, so that none could come out or go in. The city was in a state of siege, and the inspectors of quarantine surrounded it.'

Sir Moses got an appeal to all Jews in the British Empire. A new Holy Land Relief Fund raised nearly £3,000. He decided to go personally to apply the Fund. In his eightieth year, he set off with Dr. Loewe, Mr. and Mrs. Sebag and Dr. Hodgkin, who was taken ill, and died in Jaffa. Of Dr. Hodgkin, his close companion on many travels, Sir Moses wrote poignantly:

'he breathed his last in a land endeared to him by hallowed reminiscences. To one so

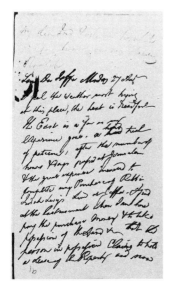

Extract from Sir Moses' diary
'The East as far as my experience goes is a hard trial of patience.'

Thomas Hodgkin's tombstone in Jaffa.

guileless, so pious, so amiable in private life, so respected in his public career, and so desirous to assist with all his heart in the amelioration of the condition of the human race, death could not have had any terror.'

He arranged for a tomb to be erected in Jaffa 'as a mark of my respect and esteem' for 'a man distinguished alike for scientific attainments, medical skill and self-sacrificing philanthropy', and was able to visit it in 1875 on his last journey abroad.

In Jaffa in March 1866 Sir Moses was met by the local Governor, the Judge, the Commander of the troops, and leaders of religious groups. He asked for detailed statistics and documents to be prepared on the conditions for Jews. While in Jaffa, there were fears that the mass of locusts forewarned further epidemics. The inhabitants had the duty of collecting and destroying as many locusts as possible before daybreak each morning. Nearing his destination, Sir Moses explained to Mr. Moore, the British Consul, that

'my principal object in visiting Jerusalem is not so much to afford pecuniary aid to the people, as to ascertain what could be done for them, so as to remove the more permanent causes of their trouble.'

On his journey he was also met by his old friend Achmet Agha Dizdar and forty horsemen sent by the Governor of Jerusalem, Izzet Pasha.

'There were to be seen all our brethren from Jerusalem who were capable of leaving the city, headed by the representatives of their synagogues, colleges and schools, all hailing my approach with the exclamation 'Bárookh Hábá (Blessed be he who cometh). What I then beheld, not without deep emotion, firmly convinced me that a sincere interest in the welfare of the Holy Land does not, and will not fail to arouse in the hearts of its inhabitants an enthusiastic acknowledgement.'

Much of his stay was spent receiving reports on the welfare of the people. With the Governor he estimated the water scarcity in the city and proposals to turn the three reservoirs into two to increase the flow from the Urtas. £200 of the Holy Land Relief Fund was devoted to this. Sir Moses augmented this with £100 of his own, gave another £100 to find a place for lepers beyond the city gates, and a further £100 for poor Jews. He inspected the Touro almshouses:

'These almshouses are situated in the most healthy part of the suburbs of the Holy City; scrupulous attention is paid to the preservation of order and cleanliness, and the inmates are cheerful and happy, devoting a portion of their time to religious observances and study; but nevertheless, not neglecting the following of industrial pursuits. Most of (them) were mechanics and apply themselves to a variety of trades. These almshouses are so highly esteemed that even many inhabitants of the city seek permission for a short sojourn there, for the recovery of their health. Some of the back offices, only intended for lumber rooms, had been actually, though without my knowledge, appropriated as dwellings for several families.'

He erected an awning for the Wailing Wall to provide shelter from rain and heat for the religious, and had meetings with leaders of the Jewish communities and representatives of charitable institutions and colleges. Decisions were made to increase the dwellings for the poor and agricultural schemes, lessen the heavy taxes, grant facilities for emigration, establish building and loan societies and obtain permission to open butchers' shops. Applications for employment in agriculture came from deputations from Safed, Tiberias and Bokea, while Sir Moses discovered that applicants for emigration merely desired temporary relief. One young widow of 22, whose husband had died of cholera and left her with three children, expressed the consensus on emigration:

'I would rather starve together with my children whilst kissing the dust in the Holy City of Jerusalem than live in plenty elsewhere.'

Tomb of the Kings and Valley of Jehoshaphat.

Sir Moses examined documents for plots of land in the suburbs of Jerusalem and memoranda on houses for sale. He went to the two synagogues attached to the Touro almshouses, approved of the intermarriages between Sephardim and Ashkenazim, and continued his promotion of the Turkish language in Jewish education.

He organised a journey to the Mount of Olives passing the Grotto of Jeremiah, the Tomb of the Kings to the Bab-el'-Asbat, crossing the valley of Kidron to the Mount:

'we had a most beautiful view of the Dead Sea, and of the wild scenery of the heights of Moab. Then we reached the Valley of Jehoshaphat and met Khasin, the sheikh of the village of Siluen, who described to me the sufferings of the Jews during the visitation of the cholera.'

He toured the new synagogue, Khoorbát Rabbi Yehooda Hakhássid, and thanked the building committee for their perseverance and skilful management. Another pleasure was to discover how useful during the cholera outbreak had been the dispensary that he had installed. He laid the foundation stone of dwellings next to the Touro almshouses and gave a further £100 each to the poor Sephardim and Ashkenazim communities, observing how the poor cared for the destitute and orphaned. He left money for each of the synagogues, colleges, schools and charitable institutions:

'I took my departure from the Holy City, more deeply than ever impressed with its sacred reminiscences and its perennial beauty, and more fervently than ever offering prayers for its future welfare.'

Within a week he was at Jaffa, on board the *Rosetta*, bound for Alexandria. He was unwell and the sea was very rough. Accompanying the travellers were 1,500 sheep, a dozen horses and numerous oxen. The ship rolled terribly, there were towering waves on deck. Some of the animals were swept overboard. Amidst the panic, Sir Moses remained on deck all night, resigned but calm. Fortunately, the voyage from Alexandria to Marseilles on the *Tanjore* proved to be a contrast. The sea was calm. Theatrical performances, dances and concerts, and two Jewish hymns were played, to the delight of Sir Moses.

Back in England he informed Lord Clarendon of the progress in land cultivation and building in Jerusalem. Miss Burdett Coutts sent him £100 towards the fund for the water supply and improved dwellings. There seemed to be no thoughts of a further visit to the Holy Land, although he was always conscious of his dedication to its future well-being. In January 1870 he heard about a dinner in honour of the Archbishop of Syra and Tenos, held in the Jerusalem Chamber at Westminster Abbey. The Dean had given a toast:

'there is a land more dear to us from our childhood even than England. There is a city more sacred even than Rome, or Geneva, or Westminster: that land is the land of the East, and that city is Jerusalem.'

Sir Moses was aroused:

'And what ought Israel to think of Jerusalem? How ought we to receive the representatives of our communities in the Holy City when they come to visit us? What ought our attachment to be to the land of our forefathers? Ought it not indeed to be at least as intense as that of the venerable Dean of Westminster? I wish every one of my young friends of the rising generation would be reminded of the words "If I forget thee, O Jerusalem, let my right hand forget its cunning."'

Two months later, he put his words into action. Reports from Jerusalem reached him of yet another season of famine, drought and ravages by locusts. He organised donations which provided aid to thousands of families. Four years later there was another famine. All his work in Jerusalem was threatened. He requested information from the towns and cities he had visited in the Holy Land. In July 1874, the London Committee of British Jews reconsidered the issue of assistance to cultivate land. Sir Moses proposed that £1 million should be obtained from Jews throughout the world within a year, and a Committee be sent to the four Holy Cities to report on projected schemes for agriculture. He was prepared to go on his seventh visit:

'We have in the four Holy Cities, artisans of almost every description. All they require is proper tools, a good supply of sound materials, to give satisfaction to their employers, and to secure for themselves the necessary remuneration, and suitable dwelling-houses.'

Retiring from the Board of Deputies in August 1874, he was invited to indicate the memorial he required. He recommended works for the improvement of Jewish life in the Holy Land. The Sir Moses Montefiore Testimonial Committee collected £12,000 which he wanted invested mainly in public works and housing in the Ohel Moshe and Mazkeret Moshe quarters. In March 1875 he sent £150 for the completion of the Touro almshouses, and resolved to go to Jerusalem once more. His energy and public spirit were now to be tested to the extreme. He wanted to confer personally with those who had written to him and those he had not had the opportunity to meet on previous visits. The whole journey was documented in a *Narrative of a forty days' sojourn in the Holy Land*, illuminated throughout by the religious spirit.

A calm sea and a blue sky gave him one of the finest voyages across the Channel in June 1875. It was ideal weather for the next three months. He was only permitted to travel short stages at a time, which gave him opportunities to ascertain from Jewish communities en route their intentions regarding Jerusalem. In Venice, he met Signora Randegger-Friedenberg who wanted to begin a women's agricultural school in the Holy Land. He put her in touch with those interested in the project. It was in Venice that Admiral Sir James Drummond warned him of another cholera outbreak in Damascus, and its imminent advance along the coast. Sir Moses considered it his duty to continue. On board the *Ettore* steamer from Alexandria he met the Danish Consul at Beirut who spoke of his commitment to colonies created in Haifa and Jaffa. To Sir Moses, it was like re-reading the Dean of Westminster's words:

'Are we to stand in the background neglecting our Talmud-Tora schools, colleges and benevolent institutions in the Holy Land, while the adherents of other creeds are actively bestirring themselves to make every possible sacrifice for the cause they advocate?'

There was also serenity for Sir Moses on this journey. He observed

'a sea as calm as a lake, not a ripple could be seen on its glowing mirror. Myriads of celestial luminaries were now emitting their silvery rays of light in the spangled canopy over us. Sure and steady our ship steered towards the coast of the land so dearly beloved. The passengers appeared to be in meditation. It was silent all around us.'

Disembarking at Jaffa he met the Vice-Consul, Signor Amzalak and remarked proudly that here was a Jew who had attained high office. He stayed at Amzalak's house. In Jaffa he inspected with satisfaction the estate of Biára, which he had bought twenty years earlier to promote agriculture. Travelling by carriage to Jerusalem, he was, however, disappointed by the state of the unrepaired roads. The compensations outweighed the disadvantages:

'I was longing to see Jerusalem. On the road I recalled to memory how much exposed the traveller was in former years to the attacks of a Bedouin or some feudal lord. Now, thanks to the protection of the Turkish Government, we do not hear of such outrages on peaceable pilgrims.'

Jews were now living in large numbers outside Jerusalem. He saw new houses, some new large buildings, a recently built synagogue and two new windmills:

'I beheld almost a new Jerusalem springing up, with buildings some of them as fine as any in Europe. I could see several very fine buildings on the Mount of Olives, many new and lofty houses.'

The Mayor of Jerusalem, Astriades Effendi, was enthusiastic about the improvements, but Sir Moses was not complacent. Dr. Loewe was instructed to inspect all land for sale outside the city, the Touro almshouses, the windmill and the estate of Kérém-Moshé-ve-Yehoodit. Sir Moses was particularly pleased with the progress of the windmill's operations which had benefited the poor and encouraged industry. He visited the synagogues and cross-questioned the managers of the various charities. He was almost as energetic as he always had been. He ordered the removal of refuse from entire quarters of the city, and asked the authorities to fill the Pool of Bethseda with pure water. Houses were whitewashed and streets cleaned—major undertakings in 1875, to minimise further cholera epidemics.

His last expedition abroad, this seventh visit to Jerusalem was a spiritual pilgrimage with a mission. His aspiration, Jews settled in agriculture, had not yet materialised, but it was also a messianic dream of a return to Zion to which Sir Moses adhered:

'I am quite certain of it; it has been my constant dream and I hope it will be realised some day, when I shall be no more. I do not expect that all Israelites will quit their abodes in those territories in which they feel happy, but Palestine must belong to the Jews and Jerusalem is destined to be the seat of the Jewish Empire.'

He reflected on his life's devotion to the Holy Land:

'The great regard I have always entertained towards our brethren in the Holy Land has, if possible, increased, so that if you were to ask me, ''Are they worthy and deserving of assistance?'' I would reply, ''Most decidedly.'' ''Are they willing and capable of work?'' ''Undoubtedly.'' ''Are their mental powers of a satisfactory nature?'' ''Certainly.'' We do not want a set of indolent people who, by poring over books, teaching the Word of God, think they are performing their duties in life, and wait for our support! The Jews in Jerusalem are more industrious than many men in Europe, but when the work does not pay sufficiently, when there is no market for the produce of the land, when famine, cholera, and other misfortunes befall the inhabitants, we Israelites must render them help, raise them from their state of distress.'

He had a coherent and practical design for future supporters; to select land outside the city, build houses, create squares and crescents with a synagogue as a central feature with a public bath and a college, and houses with a plot of ground in front to promote the cultivation of olive trees, the vine and vegetables. This would give inhabitants the taste for agriculture. Similar projects were to apply to Safed, Tiberias and Hebron.

From 1876 the Executive Committee of the Sir Moses Montefiore Testimonial promoted these objectives. They advertised for qualified people to offer their services in the Holy Land. A fund was devoted to land purchase, house building and encouraging agricultural and industrial endeavours. Two plots of land were bought outside the walls of Jerusalem. The 'Mishkenoth Israel' society undertook to build houses, synagogues and public baths, while the Committee promoted weaving, wood carving and the manufacture of tiles and bricks. In ten years it spent £6,200 on 160 houses and buildings. Jerusalem then possessed a suburb of 600 houses inhabited by nearly 4,000 Jews.

It was appropriate that this seventh visit was Sir Moses last foreign journey and closed his public career. The city where nearly half a century before he had obtained his inspiration, Jerusalem, had been the watchword of his life, a symbol of Jewish traditions and a rallying cry for humanitarian Judaism. In December 1875 a Palestine Colonization Fund had been formed by the Palestine Society, to promote the colonization of Syria and Palestine and utilise waste lands for agricultural and industrial purposes. Sir Moses responded to more appeals from the Holy Cities, sending £200 for the Jerusalem poor and £107 for the Touro almshouses in June 1877, £100 for the relief of the Moslems in Safed in April 1880 and £300 to relieve the poor after the earthquake on the island of Chios the following year. He thanked the Turkish Government for protecting the inhabitants of the Touro almshouses, the fair administration of justice in the Holy Land and for security outside the Holy City. He read about the generous facilities in America for Russian emigrants at the end of 1881 and hoped similar facilities could be secured for emigrants who selected the Holy Land for colonization. Six months later news came of the foundation of the first colony for Russian emigrants purchased near Jaffa, 'Rishon Lezion' (the Pioneers of Zion).

Throughout his ninety-ninth year what interested him most was the movement in Warsaw by the promoters of agriculture in the Holy Land, in 'Chovavey Zion' (friends or lovers of Zion). A picture of Sir Moses was sold in various countries, the proceeds spent on Jewish colonists in the Holy Land. By now there were seven colonies and Sir Moses sent contributions to each. To commemorate his centenary, a portrait of him graced the cover of the Chovavey Zion album. The inscription compared him to an angel descended on earth to protect the people of Israel, to rebuild the ancient land, to assist the unhappy and to pursue justice. In addition there were references to his journeys to help his brethren, his pilgrimages, and good deeds in the Holy Land, and the hope that if the Children of Israel follow his example, Jerusalem will rise from its ruins and the Holy Land will blossom.

Contemplating the great changes since his first visit in 1827, Sir Moses recorded that very few people in England or France had taken any interest in Jerusalem then, but by 1884 there were numerous benefactors. He was cheered and positively sustained in his last days by being told how the schemes he had initiated were prospering and of Dr. H. Adler's report of the well-being of tenants in dwellings he had promoted. Through financial and practical help he had enabled the community to grow. No other person performed a greater rôle in the development of the 'old' Jewish community in Palestine. He had endowed hospitals and almshouses, created agricultural enterprises, planted gardens, built synagogues and administered the charities of others besides his own benefactions. To the last, he kept a stone from Jerusalem under his pillow. It bore the inscription 'For thy servants take pleasure in her stones, and favour the dust thereof' (Psalm 102 Verse 17). He asked that this stone be placed under his head when he died, that his head be covered by a cap made for him in Jerusalem and for other mementoes from Jerusalem to be placed with him. The dust he had brought back from the valley of Jehoshaphat would also be placed in his coffin and some sprinkled on his face in token of his deep veneration for the 'Land of Promise'. He had striven to rehabilitate the Jewish community and, in honour of his activities, five of Jerusalem's quarters are named after him. The Sir Moses Montefiore Testimonial Fund established the building of the Ashkenazi quarter 'Mazkeret Moshe' (1882) and the Sephardi quarter 'Ohel Moshe' (1883), and later three more suburbs, 'Yemin Moshe' (1892), 'Zikhron Moshe' (1905) and 'Kiryat Moshe' (1925). These quarters nurture the memory and enshrine the significance of this man's dedication to the Jewish diaspora and his love of Jerusalem.

7. ON BEHALF OF MY BRETHREN
Italy, Morocco, Roumania, Russia, Persia

Setting sail from Dover.

Apart from his seven voyages to Jerusalem and his important interventions in Damascus and Russia in the 1840s, Sir Moses undertook crucial missions to Italy, Morocco and Roumania, as well as a second visit to Russia when he was nearly 88 years old. The missions had a similar function—to plead for the rights of individuals and to acquire government recognition of such rights. This entailed meetings with, respectively, Cardinals in Rome, the Queen of Spain, the Sultan of Morocco, Prince Charles of Roumania, Alexander II, Czar of Russia, and the Shah of Persia. The adventures which Sir Moses experienced on these missions illuminate the varying kinds of diplomacy, hardships, pleasures and diverse outcomes resulting from his indefatigable activities in these countries.

ITALY

On 24 June 1858 in Bologna, a six-year-old boy, Edgar Mortara, was taken away from his Jewish parents under the pretext of having been secretly baptised a Catholic, by his nurse when he was a year old and dangerously ill. The Mortara family submitted a memorial to the Papal Government pleading for the child's return. When this failed, Jewish and Christian communities in Europe and America were contacted.

Forced baptism and abduction shocked liberal opinion in England. Initially, the Evangelical Society and its president Sir Culling Eardley took a central rôle in arousing concern in the matter. Copies of the Mortara memorial, the Papal bull against secret baptism and an example of a previous restoration of a nine-year-old Jewish girl to her parents were forwarded to Sir Moses. The Board of Deputies, under his direction, appealed to the French and Dutch Jewish leaders and the British Government, and reported the case to the British Catholic clergy and German and American Jewish communities. An appeal was sent to Napoleon III to exercise his influence with the Papal Government. Sir Moses saw the significance of the Mortara case;

> *'the civilised world will indeed be wanting in energy and wisdom if it permit the nineteenth century to be disgraced by the retention of the child in contravention of the laws of nature, morality and religion.'*

He was requested by the Board of Deputies to go on a mission to the Pope.

Cardinal Antonelli.

Fears of attacks on the Jewish community were related by Signor Samuel Alatri, President of the community, to Sir Moses, who offered to stay in the ghetto. He went with Lady Montefiore to the Vatican to leave his visiting card at Cardinal Antonelli's apartments, on the floor above the Pope. They had to climb 190 steps up a beautiful marble staircase. Returning to their residence he heard of further attempts to incite the local population against Jews. In two synagogues children had been deliberately left in order to accuse the Jews of intended murder, and there had been attacks in the streets. Rumours of ritual murder had spread alarm and increased tensions.

Lady Montefiore was ill. Sir Moses was disheartened:

'I fear there is little hope of an audience for me with the Sovereign Pontiff.'

However, with Odo Russell he met Cardinal Antonelli, who was courteous and friendly as he listened to Sir Moses' reasons for coming to Rome and his disappointment at failing to meet the Pope. The Cardinal averred that precautions would be taken in the future to prevent a repetition but the law of the Church prevented the child from being returned to the parents. He alluded to an order that Jews should not have Catholic servants if they wanted to avoid a similar outcome.

The political situation was uncertain in Rome, with the news of war between Piedmont and Austria. Fourteen thousand Tuscan troops had gone over to Piedmont. British residents were leaving Rome. Sir Moses' companions were anxious to return to England, so he had to pay twice the cost of the fare in order to reserve berths on the *Vesuvius*, which was crowded with people leaving Italy:

' "War, war, war" was the general cry. I was quite knocked up, and obliged to lie down for some time . . . all whom I had consulted in the Mortara case agreed in the opinion that I could do nothing more, and that, in the present state of things, my remaining at Rome would in no way be useful or desirable. This journey and mission has been, on many accounts, a painful and sad trial of patience, and I may truly add of perseverance.'

He left this mission empty-handed.

Returning to England, Sir Moses thanked Lord John Russell for his assistance and reported on his mission to the Board of Deputies. It recorded its appreciation to him for his personal sacrifice in undertaking it, deplored the Pope's refusal to institute inquiries into the child's alleged baptism, and protested against clandestine baptisms. He told the Board that his age was impairing his efficiency to perform his duties, and he asked to be retired from the office of President. Yet in the 1860s and 1870s he would make eight major journeys abroad! The Mortara mission failed. The child adopted the name Pius and became a Catholic priest, but one positive outcome was the creation of the Alliance Israelite Universelle to defend Jewish rights.

MOROCCO

War seemed imminent between Spain and Morocco in 1859. The Jewish inhabitants of Tangier, fearing reprisals, fled to Gibraltar. Thousands more were expected from Morocco. Sir Moses convened a meeting of the Board of Deputies to create a Committee of Relief. In 1860 he presided at a meeting of the Morocco Committee, which agreed to send a commissioner to visit the principal towns on the coast and report on the situation of Jews so that the Committee's funds could be applied effectively. For three years Sir Moses heard little. Then, in October 1863 a letter from Tangiers detailed the tragic imprisonment of two Jews.

A Spaniard in Saffi had died suddenly. The Spanish Vice-Consul suspected

poisoning. A fourteen-year-old Jewish boy who lived with the family of the deceased, confessed under torture that poison had been administered. During the investigation he denounced ten other 'participators' in the crime. Two were condemned to death; the boy was executed at Saffi, the man sent to Tangiers for public execution, to maximise the impact of the so-called Jewish conspiracy to murder the Spaniard. Jews in Tangiers feared the worst. The other prisoners awaited their fate.

This situation was similar to that which Sir Moses had confronted in Damascus. He was invited by the Board of Deputies to proceed to Saffi. Having gained Foreign Office advice and support from the Lord Mayor of London, he left Dover on 17 November 1863 accompanied by Sampson Samuel (Secretary and Solicitor of the Board of Deputies), Dr. Hodgkin and H. Guedalla. In Madrid six days later he met the Prime Minister of Spain, the Marquis of Miraflores, who reassured him that no decision had been taken against the prisoners at Saffi, and the Queen of Spain and the King Consort, who were shocked to hear that the Spanish Consuls in Morocco were being accused of ill-treating Jews.

En route for Seville, Sir Moses travelled by rail to Santa Cruz de Mudela. In Seville he spoke to Don Antonio Merry, (father of the Spanish Minister at Tangier, Don Francisco Merry y Colon). From there he went by rail to Cadiz and then by a French steam frigate the *Gorgone* to Tangier. Dr. Hodgkin described the unusual landing:

> 'Our kind captain and his officers had ingeniously contrived, on the spur of the occasion, by the help of a mattress and cordage, a kind of portable couch or car, in which, for want of a suitable landing-place, Sir Moses might be borne over a considerable extent of shallow water between the boat and the shore. His porters and a great many of the labouring classes of Israelites were wading, and his superior size thus conspicuously moving over the water, surrounded by a shabby amphibious group, appeared to me like a travested representation of Neptune among the Tritons.'

Sir Moses received an enthusiastic welcome from the Jewish community and deputations from the Jews of Gibraltar and Mogador. The Spanish Minister consented to the immediate release of the two prisoners confined at Tangier, Shalom Elcaim and Jacob Benharrosh, and Sir Moses gave the Moroccan Minister for Foreign Affairs, Sid Mohammed Bargash, his letter to the Emperor. While in Tangier, a deputation of fifty Moors urged his intercession for the release of a Moor who had been imprisoned for two and a half years without trial on suspicion of having murdered two Jews. Sir Moses interceded and secured his release.

From Tangier Sir Moses and his party went to Gibraltar. With the aid of Earl Russell and British naval authorities, H.M.S. *Magicienne*, an Admiralty frigate, had been sent from Malta to convey him to Saffi. Part of the rudder of

Sir Moses' encampment in the Moroccan desert, 1864.

the ship broke during heavy gales. They could not land at Saffi so travelled on to Mogador where the news reached Sir Moses that the Saffi prisoners had been released. The trip from Mogador to Morocco through desert took eight days. Several of the Jewish community escorted him on the first day and stayed during the first night's encampment. The Portuguese Minister at Tangier had given Sir Moses his chaise-a-porteurs to enable him to cross the stony plains of the Moroccan interior. To this were harnessed two mules, one behind and one in front:

Encampment consists of 'from thirteen to fifteen camels, several baggage mules . . . about one hundred camp followers'.

'*During this period we were subjected to broiling sun by day, and cold and occasionally heavy dews and high winds by night. Fortunately we escaped rain; otherwise we might have been detained for days in staying to pass rivers. We were met a short distance from Morocco by a guard of honour, and we were all located in a palace of the Sultan, in the midst of a garden. The change, after sleeping under cover for so many nights, is most acceptable. The Jews here are not allowed to walk the streets except barefooted. It will be, indeed, a happy event for them, if I can induce the Sultan to do away with these degradingly distinctive marks, and also to place all his subjects, irrespective of faith, on an equal footing.*'

This last observation was to be taken literally and metaphorically! Convinced of the moral effect of his visit to ameliorate the condition of Moroccan Jews, Sir Moses thought this was confirmed by his reception by the Sultan, Sidi Mohammed Ben Abderahman Ben Hisham, with a guard of honour of 6,000 troops:

Left. Sir Moses addressing the Sultan of Morocco in the courtyard of the Imperial Palace, 1864.

Right. Sir Moses riding to meet Sultan Sidi Mohammed Ben Abderahman Ben Hisham.

'*The Royal Vice-Chamberlain with a cortège of cavalry, arrived at our place to convey us. A quarter of an hour's ride brought us to the gates opening upon an avenue leading to the court-yard before the Palace. This avenue was lined on both sides by infantry troops. We must have passed several hundreds before emerging into the open plain. There we beheld masses of troops, not less than 6000. I descended from my vehicle. We arranged*

ourselves in a line to await the appearance of the Sultan. His Majesty's approach was announced by a flourish of trumpets; he was mounted on a superb white charger. The Sultan expressed his pleasure in seeing me at his Court; he said my name was well known to him, as well as my desire to improve the condition of my brethren. He dwelt with great emphasis on his long-existing amicable relations with our country. I had the honour, at this audience, to place in the hands of His Majesty my Memorial, on behalf of the Jewish and Christian subjects of his empire.'

In his address he exclaimed that he had come with the sanction of the British Government and British Jews, to ask for protection of Christians and Jews in the Sultan's Empire, and equal rights as guaranteed in the Sultan of Turkey's firman of 1840:

'In the evening we were entertained by the Oozier with true oriental hospitality . . . we elicited from the Oozier the assurance of the Sultan's desire to protect the Jews of Morocco. We discussed the enlargement of the crowded Jewish quarters in Mogador and the grant of a house for a hospital at Tangier.'

Left. *The Firman presented to Sir Moses by the Moroccan Sultan promising to the Jews 'perfect equality with all other people'.*

Right. *A likeness of Sir Moses drawn with the text of the Deuteronomion.*

Four days later he received the Imperial edict signed by the Sultan. It promised equality in justice for all. Sir Moses was convinced that Jews would in the future enjoy security.

At his second meeting with the Sultan he was conducted round the magnificent royal gardens which consisted of lakes, vineries, orange groves and olive trees. He had another rapturous reception from the Jewish community and the Sultan gave him a magnificent pavilion tent for the journey from Morocco to Mazagan. This journey of 120 miles began with an escort of a guard of honour of horse and foot soldiers. From Mazagan, where he was given a sumptuous feast at a Jewish home, he boarded the *Magicienne* for Gibraltar. In Madrid he presented the Queen of Spain with a copy of the Sultan's decree with a Spanish translation, and after travelling by rail and carriage for 25 hours non-stop to Paris gave Napoleon III a copy of the decree.

In England, Jewish communities everywhere addressed to him a total of almost 2,000 letters of congratulation. In the House of Commons on 4 March, Layard, the Under-Secretary for Foreign Affairs, reported that

'he had received a few days previously reports from the British minister in Morocco about the marvellous success scored by Montefiore, whose generosity and humanitarian spirit cannot be overpraised, for the hardships of his long trip, undertaken when he was very

old, aimed at the very noble object of defending all the Moroccan inhabitants who do not belong to the Mohammedan faith.'

The Government had been fully in favour of the mission and praised the Sultan's edict. A resolution at the London Tavern put by Sir Anthony de Rothschild and seconded by Mr. Gladstone on 13 April 1864 underlined the Board's commendation

'that Moses Montefiore, by his philanthropic zeal in undertaking, at an advanced age, a laborius journey for the purpose of remonstrating against the cruelties inflicted on the Jews at Tangiers and Saffi, and by his successful representations to the Emperor of Morocco on behalf of all non-Mohammedan subjects of that Empire, has rendered an important service to the cause of humanity.'

This meeting thanked Earl Russell for the Government's support and the Sultan's enlightenment. Sir Moses contacted the Minister of State in Morocco to check that the edict was being put into effect by the Governors of provinces, some of whom disregarded the Sultan's commands. For the Moroccan Jews,

'Let it not be that their fond hopes are a vain shadow: that their cheering anticipations of a brighter future are a delusive dream.'

The Oozier, Sid Taib El Yaminy, the Minister of State, promised that Jewish subjects would be treated with justice and that the proceedings of officials would be rigorously monitored. Sir Moses sent an address to the spiritual chiefs and elders of the Moroccan Jews, counselling them to inculcate in their poorer and less educated brethren the necessity of obedience and respect to Moslem authorities. He believed that patience and submission to the authorities were the best means of preventing the Sultan's good intentions from being flouted by some Moslems. He was optimistic about the results:

'The Imperial edict constitutes a bright epoch in the history of that Empire and must assuredly tend to advance its prosperity.'

Sir Moses was given the freedom of the City of London:

'expressive of their approval of the consistent course you have made, of the time you have spent, and of the wearisome journeys you have endured, in order to alleviate the sufferings of your co-religionists, but at the same time to alleviate the sufferings and miseries of people of all creeds and denominations.'

He received approbation of his mission from the Queen at Windsor Castle, and praised the campaigns by the Corporation of the City of London for religious freedom, presenting them with a copy of the edict.

Its implementation proved difficult. The Sultan strictly adhered to it, but in subsequent years Sir Moses received complaints from Jewish communities of ill-treatment and oppression by local governors or military officers. Five years after the edict several Jews at Abdá were murdered and a letter was read in public to the two governors of Abdá expressing the Sultan's condemnation of the atrocities.

February 5th was celebrated each year by Sir Moses in memory of the edict. A special service and an address in Judith Lady Montefiore College, Ramsgate were performed. In 1873, because of the arbitrary conduct of a judge at Saffi, Sir Moses addressed a new petition to the new Sultan, Mooli Abd-er-Rakhman.

'Sidi Mohammed ben Sidi Tayibbi, a judge of Saffi, has ventured to oppress and ill-treat the Jews of that town, and has instigated others to injure and oppress them. I humbly entreat your Majesty to cause (his) conduct to be investigated so that all your governors, administrators and judges may know that your benevolent designs towards my brethren remain unchanged.'

Hearing of further ill-treatment of Jews, in Fez in 1877, Sir Moses prepared to go to Morocco again

Left. *Exterior of the Mausoleum at Ramsgate where Sir Moses and Lady Montefiore are buried.*

Below left. *The Holy Ark used at East Cliff Lodge before the synagogue in Ramsgate was built.*

Below right. *Interior of the Mausoleum showing the tombs of Sir Moses and Lady Montefiore.*

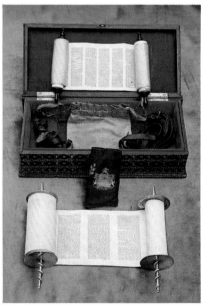

Above left. *The travelling lamp, used to light the candles for Chanucah.*

Above. *Travelling Scrolls and Tefillin in Italian velvet lined box.*

Left. *Sir Moses' Bible, a wedding present from his mother, daily prayer book and Tefillin case.*

Photographs by John R. Freeman & Co. Ltd.

Opposite in colour. *Interior of the synagogue at Ramsgate.*

'if the Board of Deputies should deem it proper to entrust me with a Mission to the Sultan, I shall regard the confidence they would thus repose in me as a high compliment and should be ready to start at a moment's notice.'

The problem was deep-rooted, but his determination to solve it was unrelenting.

ROUMANIA

In the first half of the nineteenth century the Roumanians struggled for independence from the Ottoman Empire. In 1850 when the country was divided into two principalities, Moldavia and Wallachia, a decree ordered all Jews in villages to move to towns. Thousands would thus be deprived of earning a living. Sir Moses was asked to intercede to prevent the decree but could do nothing at the time.

At the Congress of Paris in 1858 a guarantee of civil rights for the 200,000 Jews (in the population of 5 million) seemed possible. Napoleon III was the unofficial protector of the Roumanians and Baron James de Rothschild inquired about political equality for religious and ethnic minorities. However, a mixture of xenophobia and nationalism swept the region. Homogeneity required hounding out alien influences, whether Turks, Serbs, Magyars, Slavs or Jews. In September 1859, from Galatz came reports of the murder of Jews and destruction of synagogues. Sir Moses requested the British Government to instruct the Consul to protect the citizens in Galatz, but the problem was more complex.

Opposite in colour. *Olive wood pointer and Megillahs from Jerusalem.*

Opposite in colour. *Silver Tora pointers and Breast Plate for the Scroll of the Law.*

In uniting the two principalities in the state of Roumania, Alexandri Ioan Cuza had ordered a commission to prepare for Jewish emancipation. Unfortunately, he was overthrown in 1866, and the new monarch invited Bratianu to invoke nationalism and anti-semitism as a diversion from social unrest and to limit Jewish commercial competition. He stigmatised the Jews as a social wound and implored Roumanians to save the country from 'that leprosy'. Crémieux, President of the Alliance Israélite Universelle, and Sir Moses' colleague on the mission to Damascus in 1840, conferred with Bratianu who promised equal political rights. Immediately Crémieux had departed, anti-semitism burgeoned. The Government blamed the Jews for unrest, Jewish families were made bankrupt when forbidden to live in rural areas or own inns and taverns, and thousands were deported from Jassy on the pretext that they were making the city 'a dangerous focus of infection'.

Sir Moses was deluged with petitions. The Chief Rabbi of Jassy, Jesias Bhor, pleaded:

'The eyes of all Israel in the province of Moldavia are directed to you for salvation and consolation, to deliver them out of the power of their enemies. Surely the man Moses will rouse himself as a lion for the rescue of his people, as he has done in days of old.'

Sir Moses immediately communicated with the Board of Deputies:

'If, in the opinion of your Board and that of our Community, it should be considered that my presence in Moldavia might prove of utility to those who in their misery apply to us for sympathy and aid, I should feel it an imperative duty at whatever personal risk and sacrifice, to respond to the appeal.'

Prince Charles of Roumania.

His initial plan was to travel to Jassy but then he was advised to go directly to Prince Charles in Bucharest. The European governments approved his mission. Bismarck's comments were the most perceptive. He thought Prince Charles of Roumania found the ill-treatment of Jews repugnant, but was not in control of local governors. European public opinion was further shocked by the revelation of outrage at Galatz in July 1867. Ten Jews had been exported from

Jassy to Galatz and abandoned without food or shelter halfway across the Danube on a marshy island. Two of them died.

On 4 August Sir Moses was in Paris gaining the support of Napoleon III for the mission. When he was in Vienna, a telegram arrived from Mr. Halfon, President of the Comité de l'Alliance Israélite de Bucharest, strongly advising him against proceeding because he might hurt the feelings of Prince Charles, the Government and the Roumanian population. Sir Moses had promised the Jewish communities that he would plead their cause and felt he was acting on behalf of the poorer class of Jews who had publicly expressed their grievances. On 18 August he left Vienna on an Austrian steamer and reached Bucharest five days later, staying at the Hotel Ottetelechano.

The weather was oppressive; so was the situation:

'I suffer greatly by this climate; the heat of the weather deprives me of strength. Nevertheless, the hope of success cheers me. The reports constantly made to me of the serious aspect of affairs in this country, and at the intended outbreak against my co-religionists, are very alarming.'

For some, his presence in Bucharest was a provocation. On 23 August, the journal *Natiunea* contained a harangue by the editor:

'Two weeks ago we announced to our readers the arrival of a wealthy Israelite from London, Sir Moses Montefiore, and now this personage, who is in possession of the keys to all the doors of the Cabinets of Europe, actually arrived yesterday in our capital. You will indeed still have in your veins sufficient of the blood of your ancestors not to permit that the land should fall into the hands of the Hebrews! The enemies have no other design than money and thus the ruin of the simple Roumanian people. The enemies mean to transform our land into a Palestine, these bloodsuckers, the Hebrews. Awake ye Roumanians! to the duty not to allow the naturalization of the Hebrews, those outcasts. Shall you suffer political privileges to be given to the Hebrews, so that nothing will be left in your hands. Citizens of the Capital! It is incumbent upon you to call out all Roumanians for a common action, as a welcome to the noble Israelite, Montefiore, that Hebrew—whom even our Minister of State, Mr. Stefan Golesku, is said to have received at the gates of the capital with great splendour.'

The diatribe continued—demands that no Crown lands be sold, all Jews who had immigrated since 1848 and had no industrial occupation to be expatriated, and privileges granted to Jewish factory owners to be limited. The editor told the Prefecture of the intention to gather signatures to the petitions.

On 27 August Sir Moses presented his own petition to Prince Charles of Roumania. It entreated him to warn 'all evil disposed persons' not to molest Jews and thanked the Prince for enlightened sentiments of religious toleration. The following day, the editor of another journal, *Speranta*, called on Sir Moses to warn him that he had been told that Sir Moses was going to be killed. Sir Moses was more anxious about the general situation:

'I feel very weak and poorly today; the air is excessively hot, and I am vexed with sinister reports and intended outbreaks against the Jews.'

He had another meeting with the Prince who recollected his two visits to England:

'The Prince and all the party went into the garden afterwards, and I had the honour of smoking a cigar with him. Coffee, cigars and liqueurs were handed round.'

Sir Moses visited the British Consul, Mr. Green. He explained the objective of his visit—to obtain assurances from the Prince and his Government that Jews should enjoy security and be treated with justice. On returning to the Hotel Ottetelechano, a huge crowd had gathered in front of the windows of the apartments where he was staying. A table had been placed with the petitions

Sir Moses addressing the crowd from the hotel in Bucharest.

for signatures. Inside the hotel there was pandemonium. Sir Moses was told that the crowd wanted his death. He went to the window and addressed them

'Fire away, if you like. I came here in the name of justice and humanity to plead the cause of innocent sufferers.'

After a while the crowd, threatening and shouting, dispersed. Mr. Halfon, who had advised Sir Moses not to venture to Bucharest, was terrified of leaving the hotel. 'We shall all be massacred.' Sir Moses attempted to reassure him:

'I will at once order an open carriage, take a drive through the principal streets and thoroughfares, go even outside the town. Everyone shall see me; it is a holy cause; that of justice and humanity. I trust in God; He will protect me.'

His assurances seemed unwise. A few days earlier two people had been murdered in the street in broad daylight. An open carriage it was to be, with two lights in front so that Sir Moses could be seen. Mr. Halfon fled to his house. For two hours Sir Moses with others drove round the town and outside. A carriage followed them. Was he going to be murdered on the open road? Fear turned to farce when the unknown carriage was found to contain a man who wanted Sir Moses to ask Prince Charles to grant him continuance of the

Sir Moses in an open carriage.

99

privilege of lighting the town with oil-lamps! Back at the hotel, fortified by soldiers and police commissioners since the hostile demonstration, Sir Moses confined his thoughts to his diary:

'I am most anxious, weak, out of health, and vexed to the heart. No one can imagine the extreme pain of my situation. Political factions strive to create confusion by my presence in this place.'

Prince Charles' reply to his petition ignored the anti-semitism in Roumania:

'The wishes you have for your co-religionists are already accomplished. Jews are the object of my solicitude and that of my Government. Religious persecution does not exist. I respect religious liberty. All people are treated equally under the law.'

This letter was unsatisfactory and of little practical value—but it was used by Sir Moses as a starting-point for correspondence with the Prince's Ministers. He had merely sought security for Roumanian Jews:

'fully relying on the honoured words of Prince Charles I consider my object happily accomplished.'

Unfortunately, anti-semitism could not be halted by the 'word' of Prince Charles.

Having experienced oppressively hot weather and a sandstorm at Giurgevo on the return journey, he boarded the Danube steamer on 4 September. The adventures were not yet over:

'When our boat passed through the whirlpools, not far from the famous cavern 'Piscabara', we were exposed to great danger. The bed of the Danube is here formed of numerous masses of perpendicular rocks, between which it is necessary to steer with the utmost caution. There was only one narrow channel through which vessels could pass, and then only one at a time, and had ours been met by another coming in an opposite direction, they would both have been carried away by the violence of the stream, and dashed to pieces by the water rebounding from rock to rock.'

Eventually in England, a letter was awaiting him from the Portuguese and German congregations at Bucharest thanking him for his visit to 'our encampment in this wilderness'.

A very popular portrait of Sir Moses.

Mr. Halfon (who had told him not to go there, and fled from the hotel), in thanking him for £200 for distribution among the Christian and Jewish poor, was optimistic about the outcome of Sir Moses' interventions

'Since your departure, no representation or complaint has reached me from any person. I am convinced of its being a happy prelude of the fruits of your philanthropic voyage.'

The Board of Deputies acknowledged the dangers and anxieties in this arduous mission and congratulated him upon what were the hallmarks of his style of diplomacy, his perseverance, untiring energy and wise discretion. He was also honoured by the Deputy of Ramsgate who invited him to sit for his portrait, executed by S. A. Hart, R.A.

Anti-semitism did not diminish in Roumania. In January 1868 the British Consul contacted Sir Moses about another serious outbreak against the Jews at Berlad. His response was a telegram to the Chief Rabbi of Berlad urging him to appeal through the British Consul, a letter to Prince Charles and another to *The Times*, declaring that there was

'every reason to hope that Prince Charles, himself a most enlightened ruler among the Potentates of Europe, who has repeatedly expressed his disapproval of acts of injustice, will not rest until he will have secured to all irrespective of their religious convictions, full protection and the rights and privileges to which every loyal subject is fully entitled.'

The very next day, Stefan Golesku, the Minister who had given him such a warm welcome, according to the *Natiunea*, replied:

'His Highness is determined not to permit that any class of his subjects, whatever may be their religion, shall ever be molested with impunity on account of their creed, or for any other cause. Those of your co-religionists who have suffered in the troubles of Berlad will be indemnified.'

Such a promise seemed worthless when, in March, Sir Moses received a telegram from the Jewish community of Jassy relating how 31 Deputies had submitted a Bill to expel all Jews from the countryside, label transgressors 'vagabonds', prevent them buying or selling houses, farming, owning inns, contracting for any undertakings or selling beverages or food. Laws contrary to this Bill were to be abrogated. Sir Moses' intervention had been rendered fruitless in practice. Mob attacks on Jews in cities mounted in 1871 and 1872, and the Government enacted further restrictive legislation. Prince Charles was powerless to intervene.

Up to 1878, the Roumanian Government reinforced its policy denying civil and political rights to Jews, treating them as 'aliens' yet forcing them into service in the army. In 1877 in Vaslui, Moldavia, 300 Jewish families had been robbed of most of their possessions and expelled from their homes by order of the local Prefect. A fund for their relief was organised by the Board of Deputies but it only touched the surface of the problem. After the Russo–Turkish War of 1877–1878, Roumania achieved de jure independence during the Congress of Berlin, which was summoned to settle the Eastern Question. It was the scene of intense Jewish diplomatic lobbying. What was achieved was a specific clause withholding recognition of Roumanian independence until Jews had been granted equality of rights.

Sir Moses met Disraeli at Charing Cross station on the latter's return from Berlin. He thanked him for helping to insert the clause in the Treaty, and the two men, both of Italian Sephardi origin, embraced. Their differing interventions came to a sad ending. In 1880 when Roumania achieved complete sovereignty, Jews were stigmatised as 'aliens'. Barred from professions, state employment or the export trade, they suffered further disabilities in the 1890s. The Government encouraged pogroms and looting of Jewish stores and homes, precipitating further emigration, mainly to America. Balkan nationalism exacerbated the situation, and ultimately Roumanian Jews became the most wretched minority in Europe. Sir Moses' tactful and discreet diplomacy could not be repeated before the First World War.

RUSSIA AGAIN

In the first ten years of the reign of Alexander II (1855–1881), 'useful elements' among the Jewish population, those of superior financial or educational potentialities, were rewarded. They aided Russia's industrial ventures and backward rural population. The inner provinces of the Empire were opened for permanent residence to Jewish businessmen who supplied money and materials for railway construction, while doctors were needed in the army and civil life. However, the great mass of Jews remained penned up within the Pale of Settlement and all reforms were halted as a response to the Polish revolt against Russian rule. The Government became Slavophil. Jews were singled out for persecution. Informers like Jacob Brafman lobbied for anti-Jewish legislation. In 1871 the Council of State's Jewish Commission recommended the abolition of Jewish separatism. A new municipal statute restricted their participation in town government, while life for most Jews was parochial and insulated from the Russian people and language. They thought Slavic culture was primitive and their own world safe. Then, in April 1871,

Benjamin Disraeli, Earl of Beaconsfield, (National Portrait Gallery).

101

persecution against Jews in Odessa. This disturbance was quelled by troops and Sir Moses expressed confidence that the Russian Government would secure the safety of citizens:

> *'I should like to go to St. Petersburg to thank the Emperor for the prompt measure that had been taken by the Government at Odessa to put an end to the outbreak against the Jews.'*

He did not go, but the following year Jewish communities invited him to celebrate the bi-centenary of the birth of Peter the Great and present an address in person to the Czar. He travelled to Hull on 11 July. Despite news of cholera in St. Petersburg, he boarded the *Orlando* for Gothenburg. In Stockholm he met the Russian Ambassador, de Giers and the *Dagmar* steamship took him to Helsingfors, from where he travelled all night by special train to St. Petersburg. Twenty-six years since his first visit he discovered a new thriving Jewish community:

> *'Several of our brethren came to the hotel, and joined us in Sabbath prayers. I noticed among them two who had been with me on a similar occasion twenty-six years ago. At that time they were serving in the army; they are now enjoying all the advantages of free citizenship. I conversed with Jewish merchants, literary men, editors of Russian periodicals, artisans, all of whom alluded to their present position in the most satisfactory terms. All blessed the Emperor. The Jews now dress like ordinary gentlemen in England, France or Germany. Their schools are well attended, and they are foremost in every honourable enterprise destined to promote the prosperity of their community and the country.'*

Alexander II returned from army manoeuvres to meet Sir Moses in St. Petersburg at the Winter Palace:

> *'We ascended in a lift to the great ante-room of the Emperor, into which we were immediately ushered. Soon afterwards I was conducted into the presence of His Imperial Majesty, to whom I presented the address: "you, Sire, have been selected as an instrument of Providence to emancipate millions of human beings, to foster education, to*

A letter from Sir Moses from Ramsgate 29 July.

East Cliff Lodge
. Ramsgate 29 July 5643

Dear Sir

Believing that you take an interest in the welfare of our Brethren in Russia, I have much pleasure in handing you the accompanying copy of a Letter of Congratulation, which I had the honor of addressing to the Emperor on occasion of the auspicious event of his Coronation, and

His Imperial Majesty's reply to the same
The gracious reception His Majesty has given to my humble felicitations, and the kind sentiments His Excellency, the Secretary of State deigned to express towards me, I venture to regard as pleasing harbingers of His Imperial Majesty's benign intentions regarding His Hebrew Subjects; and trust, that, henceforth, they will all dwell in peace in full enjoyment of the fruit of their industry and integrity
. I am, Dear Sir
with best regards
yours truly
Moses Montefiore

encourage the arts and sciences, and to promote free intercourse between man and man, by opening the gates of your Imperial Majesty's vast Empire to persons of all religious denominations."''

Greeted by the local Jewish community Sir Moses gained the impression that the circumstances of Russian Jewry had improved. This applied to the minority in St. Petersburg despite his prognosis:

'Looking back to what the condition of our co-religionists in Russia was twenty-six years ago, and having regard to their present position, they have now indeed abundant reason to cherish grateful feelings towards the Emperor, to whom their prosperity is in so great a measure to be attributed; and if there yet remain restrictions, the hope may be surely entertained that with the advance of secular education among them those disabilities will be gradually removed.'

He left St. Petersburg and travelled all night to Königsberg. As in 1846 he stayed in Kowno and Wilna and was warmly greeted by the Jewish communities. His whole trip from Königsberg, Berlin and Hanover reinforced his confidence for the future:

'During my journey I had frequent opportunities of receiving from our brethren assurances of the rapid increase of their Synagogues, schools and charitable institutions, and as indicative of the improved spiritual and social condition of our co-religionists abroad, I may notice that amongst the many thousands of Jews with whom I came into contact, I observed the most charitable and benevolent dispositions, an insatiable thirst for knowledge, a pure and religious zeal, and a high degree of prosperity.'

On 6 September, he submitted his report on this visit to Count Brunnow. He planned to return to Russia when the Duke of Edinburgh married the Grand Duchess Marie Alexandrovna of Russia in 1873, offering to take the address of congratulations from the Board of Deputies to St. Petersburg. Count Brunnow, on becoming acquainted of his intention, persuaded him not to undergo the fatigue of travelling. He was also prepared to travel to St. Petersburg in 1879 to challenge the accusation of ritual murder brought against the Jews of Kutais in the Caucasus. He wrote to the counsel for the defence offering his services to plead the cause of the accused but the Jews were acquitted, so that journey, at the age of 95, was deemed unnecessary.

Then in March 1881 came a great shock for him; the assassination of Alexander II. He deplored this calamity without realising the appalling effect the assassination would have on Russian Jews. This would go far beyond the resources of private philanthropy and persuasion as represented by Sir Moses, who had not foreseen the Slavophilism which opposed the 'decadent' West, its materialism, constitutionalism and political methods. By 1880 the Slavic peasant communes, the Orthodox Church, autocracy and nationalism implied a new Russification policy. 'Liberalism' was stigmatised as the instrument of the Jews while the Government condoned the Press' Jew-baiting and police colluded in anti-Jewish riots. In 1881 Jewish homes and shops were looted and the Government initiated an investigation into injurious Jewish economic activities. Legal disabilities on Jews paralysed their communities and the May Laws of 1882 obliterated Jewish rights. The freedoms won in the 1860s vanished.

From Russia hundreds of letters reached Sir Moses describing these attacks. Meetings were held in London, Manchester, Liverpool and Birmingham, on the continent of Europe and in America to consider the tragedy. The Board of Deputies and the Anglo–Jewish Association asked Lord Granville at the Foreign Office to protest, but he thought the problem was with the Russian masses not their Government. Sir Moses' viewpoint was different but equally unrealistic. He held to the conviction that the Czar was the key to the solution of persecutions:

> *'The Prime Minister assured me, in the presence of three or four Ministers of State that the Russian Jews, if qualified by their abilities and moral character, could attain any high position in the Empire. I am fully convinced that it is only by mild and judicious representation that you have a chance of your application reaching the throne of the Emperor. If it be thought advisable, I am quite ready to go again to St. Petersburg. If necessary, I will be carried there. Take me in my carriage to the train, put me on board ship, then again in the train, and when in St. Petersburg I will be carried into the presence of the Emperor. Nothing shall prevent me from serving my unfortunate brethren if I can be of use to them.'*

The persecutions increased apace. A British Relief Committee, formed to aid Russian Jews, included Lord Shaftesbury, Charles Darwin, Matthew Arnold and Cardinal Manning. A meeting in the Egyptian Hall at the Mansion House raised £108,759 for relief and permanent emigration from Russia. In gratitude Sir Moses sent £500 to the building fund of the City of London College. His name was greeted with enthusiasm at the Mansion House. In his ninety-ninth year Sir Moses congratulated Czar Alexander III on his coronation and reminded him of the previous Czar's sentiments of paternal love towards all loyal subjects, irrespective of creed and nationality, but anti-semitism had taken hold of the Russian Empire.

A portrait of Sir Moses with his signatures.

PERSIA

> *'Alas, I am not yet finished with one effort in favour of our brethren when a new misfortune occurs.'* (Sir Moses Montefiore to Dr. Louis Loewe, 1866)

Sir Moses penned these words in reference to the outbreak against Jews at Balfaroosh in Persia. They offer a leitmotiv to all his endeavours. He had received descriptions from Hamadan, Persia, of the ill-treatment of the Jews in 1860 and entreated the British Government to intervene for their protection.

Five years later the Jewish community there were again suffering from persecution and appealed for his intercession with the Shah. The news disturbed Sir Moses

> *'I could not sleep last night for thinking of our poor suffering brethren in Persia.'*

He resolved to go there.

At the Foreign Office he told Austen Layard his intention was to obtain a firman from the Shah. Mr. Alison, British representative at the Court in Teheran, was contacted. Sir Moses was set to leave on 1 May but Layard warned against such a long and dangerous journey. His alternative was a letter to the Shah explaining that Sir Moses had obtained firmans from the Sultan at Constantinople in 1840 and the Sultan of Morocco in 1864 and to petition him for a similar edict.

Acting on this advice, Sir Moses sent his petition via Lord Russell to Mr. Alison, and relinquished his planned journey. He heard nothing for nine months. Then in January 1866 Foreign Office sources claimed that the grievances by the Persian Jews were about to be remedied, the Shah being unaware of any oppressions:

> 'His Majesty has addressed an autograph letter to the Sipeh-salar, in which he signifies to his Prime Minister that it has come to his knowledge that his Jewish subjects suffer from oppression; and that being contrary to his wishes, the Sipeh-salar is strictly enjoined to see that the Jews are henceforward treated with justice and kindness.'

All seemed fine, until despatches from Mr. Alison in Teheran brought another account of attacks on Jews in Benfarouch. The head of the Moslem population had declared that he was king and no Jew would remain alive. The Shah's officer had been attacked. Jews were homeless and starving. The Shah's authority had disappeared. Sir Moses again asked the Foreign Office if he could go to Persia. This time, a Mr. Hammond told him it was out of the question. His presence there would do no good. In compensation, Lord Clarendon sent Mr. Alison a telegram to the Shah which demanded that those who had committed the outrage should be punished. The situation did not improve. Sir Moses received further reports on Hamadan from Mr. Alison;

> 'The Jews are this year much more ill-treated than last year. Many have run away from this province.'

During the next three years complaints of oppression continued to arrive from Persia. Forced labour, excessive taxes and loss of inheritance rights were particularly onerous.

In June 1871, Captain Henry Jones, the British Consul-General at Tabriz, contacted Sir Moses about the famine in Persia and the desperate poverty of the 300 Jewish families in Shiraz. The Persian Government would not intervene. Sir Moses sent £100 to be distributed among Jews, Christians and Moslems in Shiraz, but also commented that it was 'a matter of deep regret' that oppressions continued despite the Shah's edict. The British Board of Deputies requested Jewish congregations to aid the sufferers. In December another telegram from the Secretary of the Relief Committee at Ispahan estimated that 1,200 of 1,700 in the Jewish community were starving.

Subscriptions to the fund for the relief of the famine-stricken Jews poured in. £10,850 was distributed in Shiraz, Ispahan, Hamadan and Bagdad. Appeals for rescue from oppressing governors and officials mounted, so, in 1871, Sir Moses petitioned the Shah again reminding him of the 1866 edict. When he heard from Teheran in mid-February 1872 that famine was still rife in Shiraz, Hamadan and Ispahan, he made his third attempt to go to Persia. The Foreign Office, through Mr. Hammond, again refused to permit the journey:

> 'When I said I was going by way of Egypt he said jestingly that the British Consul had great power and he would put me in prison, and in Egypt there was no Magna Carta. I ought not to go. And what did my nephew, Mr. Joseph Meyer Montefiore, say to it? he asked. I replied that my nephew said it was evident I wished to be buried in Persia.'

Lord Granville was prepared to give letters of introduction but tried to dissuade him. Sir Moses was adamant.

By May, all preparations for this visit to Persia had been made. News that the interior of Persia had been 'overrun with bands of marauders', at last compelled him, reluctantly, to abandon his plan, although the Persian Relief Fund had yielded nearly £20,000 by December 1872.

His final opportunity occurred when the Shah came to England in June 1873. Buckingham Palace was the venue. Sir Moses presented a memorial to the Shah soliciting protection for Jewish subjects. The Shah responded that he would order that no undue injustice should be done to Jews.

The Persian Minister in London later wrote that the Shah always treated his subjects with solicitude regardless of creed, and Sir Moses had rightly characterised Jewish citizens as loyal, peaceable and industrious. This correspondence was forwarded to the Jewish communities in Persia, a scroll containing this information affixed to the main entrance of synagogues. Persecution did not evaporate, yet when the Jews of Zargkoon were intimidated to renounce Judaism, the Foreign Office, urged by Sir Moses, successfully intervened and the situation was ameliorated. That was in 1877, the last contact he had with one of the countries he did not visit.

A letter to Sir Moses from the Shah of Persia while he was staying at Buckingham Palace. Sir Moses had a lithograph made of this letter, translated into Persian, Hebrew and Arabic.

8. DEVOTION TO THE FAITH

In a sermon at the Bevis Marks synagogue celebrating the centenary of Sir Moses, the Chief Rabbi, Dr. Hermann Adler analysed the motivation behind the extraordinary tenacity, consistency and assiduity displayed by Sir Moses in his public activities:

> *'Whence came it that one not dowered with the gift of tongues, nor trained in any school of diplomacy, could hold his own against the ablest statesman, that he could plead, with a voice that never faltered, before the mightiest potentates of earth? He has revealed the secret to his intimate friends. He has oft-times said: ''I never approached these audiences without ejaculating the prayer from the depth of my heart, 'O God, be Thou with my lips!' '' And having breathed forth this passionate supplication to the King of Kings, he stood fearlessly before the rulers of earth. He delivered his message to them, and was not ashamed. The centenarian is essentially a prayerful man.'*

This was the essence of Sir Moses. What made him pre-eminent was his combination of British patriotism and devotion to Judaism. Throughout his life, his religion was supportive and inspirational. He delighted in the practices of Judaism and inspired self-respect in Jews.

In his youth, Sir Moses was fortunate in having as his tutor and mentor in religious matters his uncle Moses Mocatta, who excelled in Hebrew and Jewish literature and was the author of several books on Judaism. At the age of twenty Sir Moses acquired his life commitment to Jewish public service from the traditions of the Bevis Marks synagogue. In 1804 he was made a Yahid (an assessed member of the congregation) before the usual age of possible admittance at twenty-one. As an active and regular participant in the synagogue, every morning at seven o'clock he attended the services and offered up his prayers. He served all the various offices connected with administration. Moseh de Joseph Eliaha Montefiore, as he was known in the synagogue records, became in 1808, one of the active brothers of Lavadores who performed the last rites (an honour given only to the most respected members). In 1814 he became the treasurer (Gabay), an office he held when Isaac D'Israeli refused to pay the finta (membership fee) and seceded from the

The interior of Bevis Marks synagogue.

Jewish community. In 1815 he became the chairman (and in 1816 treasurer) of the Beth Holim hospital; in 1818 he was elected President and in 1819 warden (Parnas); this was the year in which the wardens of Bevis Marks decided that henceforth the official language of their records should be English instead of Portuguese. He later became Governor of the Terra Sancta, of the hospital burial society and theological college, Beth Hamedrash, and attended meetings of the synagogue regularly thereafter.

Sir Moses celebrates the Festival of Tabernacles at East Cliff Lodge, Ramsgate.

His marriage to Judith Cohen in 1812 intensified his devotion to the faith. Her birthday was celebrated in October at East Cliff Lodge during the Tabernacle Holidays. As a Sephardi he overcame a prejudice when he married an Ashkenazi Jewess. It became a maxim of his life to provide equally for Ashkenazim and Sephardim communities, as in his building projects in Jerusalem. Judith Cohen shared his religious fervour, which was central to her own family. She recalled that as a young girl she was reciting the Lamentations of Jeremiah when Admiral Sir Sidney Smith was visiting. She told him 'This is the anniversary of the destruction of Jerusalem, which is kept by conforming Jews as a day of mourning and humiliation. We treasure the memory of it as a bright example to ourselves and to all following generations, how to fight and to sacrifice our lives for the land in which we were born and which gives us shelter and protection.' At her graveside in 1862 the Chief Rabbi praised her commitment to her faith: 'Possessed of a refined mind, of the most cultivated taste, she still, in a quiet unassuming way, devoutly fulfilled the duties of a Jewish wife. Never, not even during severe illness, did she neglect to light the Sabbath lamp—she who was herself the light of her home.'

Sir Moses and Lady Montefiore were orthodox and observant Jews in private and in public. They prayed each day. They abstained from food forbidden to Jews. They fasted on each Day of Atonement, regardless of where they were, in whichever country they might be at the time. They also lit the Sabbath candles, even if they were in the desert or travelling at sea. They never overlooked the minutiae of religious observance. It was a delight for them. In England, on the Sabbath, they walked from their West London home to Bevis Marks synagogue, having to rise very early because they wished to be seated before prayers commenced. (Sir Moses even walked from Smithambottom in Surrey to the city, a five hour walk, to avoid breaking one of the

The Kiddush cup used by Sir Moses for the blessing of the wine on the Sabbath Eve.

commandments by riding in a carriage on the Sabbath.) He was once asked 'If the commandments of Judaism and Christianity are the same, wherein lies the difference?' To which he replied: 'We obey the commandments.'

The Montefiores always adhered to the strict observances of their faith. In his business years, however profitable or urgent the matter may have been, when he had to prepare for Sabbath or other religious observations, Moses left his office, and walked the six miles home. On the anniversary of the death of his father in 1804 he spent morning and evening in synagogue, visited his tomb, distributed money to the poor and passed the whole day in fasting and religious meditation. The Montefiores provided a centre for Jewish life in London, and after 1833, in Ramsgate. From 1830 they held a regular weekly gathering with close friends and two Rabbis (who were versed in the Law of Moses, Hebrew and theological literature) for conversations.

In their Diaries, the sustenance and joy which Judaism gave them is paramount. Moses recorded in 1820:

'With God's blessing—Rise, say prayers at 7 o'clock. Breakfast at 9. Attend the Stock Exchange, if in London, 10. Dinner, 5. Read, write and learn if possible, Hebrew and French, 6. Read Bible and say prayers, 10. Then retire. Monday and Thursday mornings attend the Synagogue.'

In October 1821 he observed his appreciation:

'I was present, on the Feast of Hanukah (the anniversary of the victory of the Maccabees), at a discourse delivered by the spiritual head of the congregation in the College of the Spanish and Portuguese Hebrew Community. The interest was greatly enhanced by the completion of the study of one of their theological books in the presence of all the students.'

On 5 September 1857, the Day of Atonement, he and his wife attended the services at Bevis Marks from 7 a.m. to 6.30 p.m. He relates the great pleasure he felt at having been called upon during the service to read publicly the chapter referring to the day from an ancient scroll of the law presented by his grandfather to this synagogue. He delighted in intoning the services and in his sonorous voice chanting its hymns with fervour.

Nourished in the Judaic traditions and sustained by the ceremonials Sir Moses and Lady Montefiore travelled abroad. Wherever they went, whenever they rested, they would visit and pray in the local synagogue and distribute money for the poor. Sir Moses took on his travels his sefer-torah, teffilen, menora and prayer-book. He also took his own Jewish cook (shochet), Mr. Tarachi, to prepare kosher meat, and they supplied their own utensils. Before undertaking any journey abroad, the Montefiores would first visit the synagogue for blessings. On arrival they offered 'praise for having preserved us from so many perils'. Immediately they returned they would attend synagogue to offer up prayers for their safe return. When travelling to the Holy Land they would frequently dismount and read from the Bible. On the first sight of Jerusalem, Sir Moses records: 'dismounting once again we recited prayers, giving thanks to God for having brought us safely to Jerusalem'.

Travelling through France on their first visit to Jerusalem, Sir Moses was grieved that he could not practise his religion at one point: 'I am mortified that though there are many Jews in this place there is no synagogue. No meat prepared according to Jewish law can be obtained. We could manage with fish and vegetables, but I regret not being able to join public worship on Sabbath. Tomorrow will be the first time we have omitted doing so since we left London. I shall be happy if it is the last.' After his visit to Jerusalem he commemorated his return with a banner on his coat of arms bearing the word 'Jerusalem' in

Hebrew. In his Passover prayer-book he reproduced an extract from his journal which described a storm at sea on their journey when he threw into the sea a piece of Matsah 'whereupon the stormy sea became tranquil', and he gave thanks to God for his preservation.

Sir Moses and his wife had an unswerving faith in the literal fulfilment of the sacred prophecies, in the ultimate restoration of Israel to its ancient land. Arriving in Jerusalem in 1839 Sir Moses uttered a prayer:

'The Lord God of Israel be praised and thanked for permitting our feet to stand a second time within thy gates, O Jerusalem, may the city soon be rebuilt in our days. Amen.'

Lady Montefiore composed the following in remembrance:

'What the feelings of a traveller are, when among the mountains on which the awful power of the Almighty once visibly rested, and when approaching the city where he placed his name; whence his law was to go forth to all the world; where the beauty of holiness shone in its morning splendour; and to which even in its sorrow and captivity, even in its desolation, the very Gentiles, the people of all nations of the earth look with profound awe and admiration—Oh! What the feelings of the traveller are on such a spot. Dismounting

A portrait of Sir Moses.

110

A portrait of Lady Montefiore.

from our horses, we sat down and poured forth the sentiments which so strongly animated our hearts in devout praises to Him whose mercy and providence alone had thus brought us, in health and safety, to the city of our fathers.'

In Jerusalem, she promoted the formation of a Ladies' Charity for the relief of the sick, and in a farewell address by the Portuguese and German congregations of Jerusalem she was acclaimed: 'By the blessing of the Almighty did Moses obtain the accomplished, honoured and most virtuous Lady Yehoodit (Judith).' In Safed, she took part personally in the ceremony of receiving a new scroll of the Law in the Synagogue and in another synagogue she decorated the scroll during divine service.

After the Damascus Mission, wherever Sir Moses travelled he was greeted by crowds of brethren, and when he departed further crowds accompanied him out of towns. Typical were the prayers and thanksgiving in all the synagogues on his return from Russia in 1846 with numerous addresses from the congregations—all preserved in the College he created at Ramsgate.

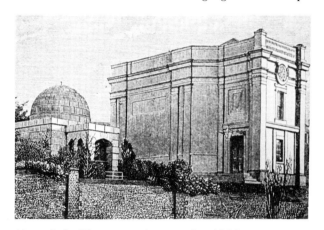

Above Left. *The synagogue in Ramsgate and the Mausoleum.*

Above Right. *The dedication of the Ramsgate synagogue.*

In 1831, to commemorate the first visit to the Holy Land, he laid the foundation stone of his synagogue at Hereson, Ramsgate, placing some Terra Sancta brought from Jerusalem near where the Holy Ark would be built. In May 1833 the synagogue in the grounds of East Cliff Lodge, was inaugurated. Invitations were sent to the Sephardim and Ashkenazim congregations, officers of the synagogue and two hundred friends and relatives to dedicate the synagogue on 16 June. It was a magnificent occasion, with music, singers, fireworks, balloons and 4000 lamps to illuminate the gardens. The dedication commenced:

'Open unto us the gates of righteousness, we will enter them and praise the Lord.'
'This is the gate of the Lord, the righteous shall enter therein.'

The doors were opened and the congregation exclaimed upon entering:

'How goodly are thy tents, O Jacob! thy tabernacle, O Israel! O Lord, I have ever loved the habitation of thy house and the dwelling-place of thy glory. We will come unto Thy Tabernacle and worship at thy footstool.'

The readers and choristers then sang:

'Blessed be he who cometh in the name of the Lord: we will bless ye from the House of the Lord.'

The procession, carrying sepher torahs, made seven circuits round the synagogue reciting psalms. Sir Moses offered up Hebrew prayers:

'Almighty God! whose eyes are upon all the ways of the sons of men, and by whose will their paths are established; wherewith shall I come before thee, how shall I acknowledge the kindness Thou has shown me from my youth? How great the goodness Thou has

111

vouchsafed unto me, in granting the fulfilment of the ardent desire Thou didst awaken in my heart and in that of the companion of my life, to visit the inheritance of our forefathers, to traverse the sea and behold the Holy Land, a land which is under Thy special providence. Thou has protected us on our departure and aided our return; our steps failed not, we have passed through the Land, our feet have stood within thy gates, O Jerusalem!'

There were also hymns and a prayer for the Royal Family. Two months later, the Montefiores returned to Ramsgate:

'We had the happiness of attending our Synagogue, morning, afternoon and evening. Thanks to Heaven for a very happy day. Our Synagogue looked like Paradise. I pointed out to my dear Judith the spot, not more than ten or fifteen steps from the Synagogue, in which I should like my mortal remains to rest when it shall please the Almighty to take my soul to Eternal Glory, should I depart this world at or near East Cliff.'

Although he attended the dedication of the new synagogue at Great St. Helens in 1838, donated £200 for the repair of Bevis Marks in 1842, gave £500 towards the construction of a new synagogue in the West End in 1846, laid the foundation stone of Canterbury synagogue the following year, and was present at the laying of the foundation stone of the first Portuguese Synagogue in Manchester in 1873, the only experience to equal that of 1833 in Ramsgate occurred when he was in Pisa twenty-five years later:

'The Synagogue was very well attended, both by males and females, and it is one of the handsomest little Synagogues I have ever seen. I wish I had seen it before I built one at Ramsgate. I would have gladly adopted the plan. It will accommodate three hundred persons, and has a splendid ark, containing the sacred scrolls of the Pentateuch. My godfather, Moses Haim Racah, of blessed memory, attended this Synagogue when residing at his country house at Pisa. He was a very liberal contributor to the Synagogue and charities at Pisa. I consider myself most fortunate in having been blessed on my coming into the world with such excellent friends as my godfather and godmother. My godfather continued a sincere friend to my dear parents to the end of his life. Peace to his soul.'

The Prayer Shawl and Tefillin.

A portrait of Sir Moses.

Many of Sir Moses' charitable activities were connected with Bevis Marks synagogue. In 1823 he presented it with thirteen almshouses for the congregational poor. On the Day of Atonement the previous year he had given £140 for Jewish charitable institutions for his appreciation of the synagogue service. In 1831 one finds him attending a meeting of the Board of Representatives of the Jewish community to supervise the sanitary conditions of the Jewish poor, and he contributed generously to funds enabling the Board to purchase warm clothing and blankets. In 1861 on the day of the Fast of Esther he attended divine service at Bevis Marks and distributed gifts among the pupils and on his 79th birthday he sent £79 to the Spanish and Portuguese community for distribution among 79 families. On his annual visits to the Spanish and Portuguese Congregational schools at Purim time, on the occasion of the distribution of prizes, he would deliver a short speech and give each of the 300 pupils a newly-minted silver coin, with the greeting 'I wish you a merry Purim'. He also gave a £50 prize to the best Hebrew scholar in the Merchant Taylor Company schools in 1837, which had mounted to 100 guineas by 1849. He also contributed a great deal to the Jews' Free School (he was its President) and Jews' College, a theological seminary, which opened in 1856.

In his diaries there are references each month to small and large amounts of money he has received from Jews throughout the world, for distribution to the poor at his discretion. This is an eloquent testimony to the reverence in which he was held. His compassion was epitomised in his visits to the houses of the Jewish poor. One such visit took place on 14 April 1829:

'We were, from soon after 10 in the morning till 5 p.m., about Petticoat Lane and the alleys. We witnessed many very distressing scenes: parents surrounded by children, frequently 6 or 7, seldom less than 2 or 3, with little or no fire or food, and scarcely a rag to cover them; without bed or blanket, but merely a sack or rug for the night, a bed being almost out of the question. Few had more than one room, however large the family. The rent was from 1s. 6d. to 3s. per week. Of those who had two rooms, the upper one was most miserable, scarcely an article of furniture. In fact, the distress and suffering appeared so great, that we could not refrain from giving what money we had in our pockets.'

Distribution of alms to the poor and the sick was part of the daily life of Sir Moses and Lady Montefiore.

As President of the London Committee of Deputies of British Jews from 1835 to 1874 he became the spokesman for the community. It also gave him the right to plead for less favoured Jews everywhere. Some were in England as has been acknowledged. Others were just across the Channel. The Montefiores were in Nice in 1838 where Lady Montefiore empathised with the struggles of the local Jewish community:

'The members of our community are subject to much oppression, and many disadvantages. How long will the powerful oppress the weak, and endeavour to stifle the energies of their fellow beings? One consolation remains under such a state of things. Conscientious feelings, well maintained under oppression, ever excite the sympathy and admiration of independent and virtuous minds.'

Even for a wealthy, privileged and honoured person, as Sir Moses was in England, he had to defend his right to be a strictly conforming Jew in public office, when he became Sheriff of London and Middlesex:

'I will not deviate from the injunctions of my religion; let them call me a bigot if they like; it is immaterial to me what others do or think in this respect. God has given man the free will to act as he may think proper. He has set before him life and death, blessing and curse. (Deut. 30:15). I follow the advice given in Holy Writ, and choose that which is considered life, which is accounted a blessing.'

Invited to official functions which clashed with holy days he simply declined to attend, because 'My duty to God, and my respect for our holy religion are above all other duties, and I must give up my official occupations for these days.'

On religious matters Sir Moses deferred to the Chief Rabbi. This was particularly the case in the debate over the Reform Judaism movement from 1841. He upheld the religious tenets of Israel, as revealed in the Code of Sinai: 'They are to show our wisdom and understanding in the sight of nations'. He believed that a Reform Synagogue would have a deleterious effect on the cohesion and identity of the community, in terms of the solemnization of marriages, dietary laws and observance of the Sabbath.

In 1858 Jews were at last admitted to sit as Members of Parliament, and Sir Moses had served for 30 years on the London Committee of Deputies of British Jews. He was congratulated

'for the faithful, zealous and impartial manner in which you have fulfilled your duties and to one whose uniform kindness and courtesy, and whose veneration for the religion of his forefathers, has won for him the esteem, the admiration and the love, not alone of the Jews of this happy land, but of those of the civilised world.'

On his retirement, on 4 August 1874, the Board commended him for his services:

'Sir Moses Montefiore's lengthened association with the Board, his exalted character, his potent influence in the councils of monarchs and of ministers, and the rare judgement and

*tact which he exhibited in directing the affairs of the Board. By his unremitting and successful efforts on behalf of the weak and persecuted, (he) has kindled a spirit of enlightenment and toleration in foreign countries, which has already led to a material improvement in the condition of oppressed **nationalities**. That by these means Sir Moses Montefiore has acquired for himself a glorious and imperishable renown, and the enduring gratitude of his co-religionists.'*

Left. *The interior of the Mausoleum showing Lady Montefiore's tomb.*

Right. *The Judith, Lady Montefiore Theological College on the right, synagogue in the centre and the Mausoleum on the left.*

Twelve years earlier, on the eve of the Jewish New Year, Lady Montefiore died. She was buried at East Cliff. The Chief Rabbi spoke of her services to humanity, promotion of good causes and the constant companion of her husband on philanthropic missions abroad. The service was held in the synagogue. Sir Moses had considered having her remains taken to Jerusalem and interred in the valley of Jehoshaphat. Instead, he decided to build over her grave a mausoleum similar in shape to the Tomb of Rachel in the Holy Land (which she had ordered to be renovated twenty years before and to which they had added a chamber). In her memory he distributed 350 gifts to synagogues, charities, schools and friends and founded scholarships and prizes for children at Jewish schools. The Jewish community in England founded the Judith, Lady Montefiore Convalescent Home at South Norwood.

In 1864 Sir Moses planned a college in Ramsgate for the study of theology to be built near the synagogue in memory of his wife. In June 1865 he laid the first foundation stone of the College. He selected the fittings for its ten apartments, library and reading room, and deposited documents, mementoes, books and souvenirs from his own collection. The Judith, Lady Montefiore Theological College was opened in 1869 for rabbis, as a place of learning and prayer, a centre of Jewish scholarship in the old tradition:

'as a memorial of Sir Moses' sincere devotion to the law of God as revealed on Sinai and expounded by the revered sages of the Mishna and the Talmud, and as a token of his love and pure affection to his departed consort, Judith Lady Montefiore, of blessed memory, whose zeal and ardent attachment to the religion of her forefathers adorned all her actions in life.'

The Yeshibath Ohel Moshé ve-Yehudith was a tribute to the religion which had enhanced their marriage for fifty years. Dr. Loewe was made the Principal of the College and Sir Moses laid down the guidelines:

'It is my distinct wish that admission as members of the College should be given to all Israelites, from whatever part of the globe they may happen to come, provided their learning and moral and religious character qualify them for the College.'

Two letters written by Sir Moses in 1880, when he was nearly 96 years old, exemplify his devotion to his faith whatever the conditions. To Baron von Bleichröder, who had informed him of the Anti-Semitic Leagues in Berlin, he espoused optimism:

'I entertain the hope that by prudence and discretion on our part, and increased enlightenment based on principles of humanity among non-Israelites, an improvement in the condition of our brethren will ultimately be effected. In the meanwhile we must not relax our earnest activity, and when occasion requires it, hold up high the banner of our religion, for we must always bear in mind that "it is not by might nor by power that Israel prevails, but by the Spirit of God, the Lord of Hosts." '

In a letter to a totally different environment, Philadelphia and the journal 'Jewish World', he thanked them for their generosity:

'I am prompted to address you by a desire of manifesting to you appreciation of the important service you render to all Hebrew communities, when recalling to their memory the comforting assurance that "the Guardian of Israel neither slumbereth nor sleepeth"; that He shows mercy to the innocent sufferer at times when all hope has been abandoned by him; and that the Omnipotent will never withdraw His protecting grace from all who strictly abide by the law He revealed on Sinai. The Hebrew communities in America are pre-eminently distinguished by that characteristic trait of Israel. On all occasions, when the cry of anguish reaches their ear, promptly and most generously they offer their noble contributions to assuage the sufferings of the brother. And I ascribe the cause of it to their innate feeling of benevolence, intensely aroused by the eloquent addresses they hear from men of great learning and piety.'

In the Times obituary for Sir Moses, devotion to the faith was the major theme:

'When he no longer possessed the energy for conversation he was sometimes heard repeating under his breath verses in Hebrew from the Psalms, and it may truly be said that his last thoughts were occupied with the duties of piety, loyalty and benevolence, which it has been his aim during the century to fulfil. To the Jews it may well seem as if with him the central pillar of their temple had fallen; but those who calmly contemplate his life will understand that the example of his useful and benevolent career has done its work.'

On 5 August 1885, Dr. Hermann Adler concluded in his Bevis Marks sermon, 'In Memory of the late Sir Moses Montefiore', the ultimate tribute:

'He was one raised above his fellows by the services he rendered his community and mankind at large; great in his perfervid and single-hearted love of humanity, great in his devotion to his ancestral faith. If I were asked to indicate the keynote of his life, the characteristic which gained for him the affection and reverence of all classes and creeds, I would say that it was his tenacity of purpose, his unshaken consistency, the dignified firmness with which he persevered in the line of conduct he had struck out for himself, the endurance with which he laboured for the good of mankind even unto the end, the persistence with which the obligations of loyalty, piety and benevolence engaged his thoughts to the last. He did not allow himself to become a waif and stray, driven hither and thither by every wind of doctrine, but having grasped that which he felt to be the truth, he adhered to it and practised it. Imbued with the vivid belief in the eternally binding force of the precepts of Judaism, he did not turn from them. They were the joy of his life.'

9. CENTENARY CELEBRATIONS

As Sir Moses Montefiore entered his hundredth year, extraordinary festivities exploded in London and Ramsgate. From July 1883 numerous letters, poems, works of art and books arrived at his London home from all over the world. 24 October was the last day of the Feast of Tabernacles, and on this festival Sir Moses had been for fifty years the Hatan Torah (Bridegroom of the Law) in his synagogue when in England.

After morning service in the synagogue, he welcomed relatives and friends to lunch at East Cliff, while in London rabbis extolled his noble life. Under his bedroom window, on the lawn, sixty people sang hymns and songs composed specially for him. While he was sitting listening a special telegram arrived from Queen Victoria with the message:

Left. *The service at Bevis Marks synagogue to commemorate the 100 years of Sir Moses.* (Illustrated London News Nov. 1st 1884).

Right. *The telegram from Queen Victoria on entering his 100th year. Sent fom Balmoral, 1883.*

'I congratulate you sincerely on your entering into the hundredth year of a useful and honourable life.'

Hundreds of other telegrams were arriving in many different languages from all over the world, but Sir Moses immediately requested that the singers offer the National Anthem. There were other telegrams from Edward, the Prince of Wales and the Duke of Edinburgh.

The local post office had to employ extra staff to cope with the mass of gifts of fruit, flowers and works of art to honour Sir Moses' hundredth year. Between 24 October and the official public celebration on 8 November numerous visitors came to pay their respects. Deputations from towns, charities, financial and scientific institutions brought congratulations and were entertained by Sir Moses and his relatives Mr. and Mrs. Sebag and Mr. and Mrs. Guedalla. Extra trains were run from London and towns in Kent to transport the crowds to Ramsgate to share the special day. Ramsgate and all the neighbouring towns were treated to a general holiday. The shops and schools were closed. The streets were decorated with flags; triumphal arches had been constructed with inscriptions offering good wishes to Sir Moses, and street lamps were emblazoned with the initials 'M.M.' in English and Hebrew letters of gold. Even the ships in the harbour were decked with flags and salutes were fired.

Thousands of visitors arrived by train for the occasion and one hundred extra policemen were drafted in to organise the crowds. Ramsgate's streets

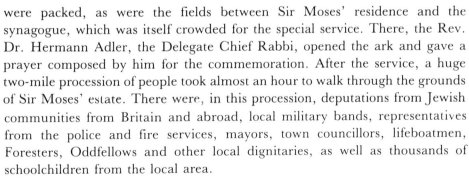

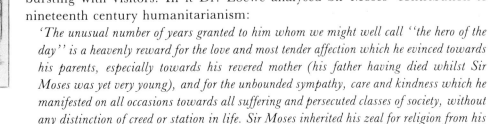

'The Montefiore Celebration at Ramsgate' (Illustrated London News Nov. 17th 1883).

were packed, as were the fields between Sir Moses' residence and the synagogue, which was itself crowded for the special service. There, the Rev. Dr. Hermann Adler, the Delegate Chief Rabbi, opened the ark and gave a prayer composed by him for the commemoration. After the service, a huge two-mile procession of people took almost an hour to walk through the grounds of Sir Moses' estate. There were, in this procession, deputations from Jewish communities from Britain and abroad, local military bands, representatives from the police and fire services, mayors, town councillors, lifeboatmen, Foresters, Oddfellows and other local dignitaries, as well as thousands of schoolchildren from the local area.

All the sections of the procession halted when they reached the balcony on which Sir Moses stood. They lowered their flags and cheered him. He lifted his cap and waved in response. After this immense procession, he received more deputations. In the evening, Dr. Loewe, principal of the Judith, Lady Montefiore Theological College, gave an address in the lecture hall which was bursting with visitors. In it Dr. Loewe analysed Sir Moses' contribution to nineteenth century humanitarianism:

'The unusual number of years granted to him whom we might well call "the hero of the day" is a heavenly reward for the love and most tender affection which he evinced towards his parents, especially towards his revered mother (his father having died whilst Sir Moses was yet very young), and for the unbounded sympathy, care and kindness which he manifested on all occasions towards all suffering and persecuted classes of society, without any distinction of creed or station in life. Sir Moses inherited his zeal for religion from his

117

ancestor (Joseph Montefiore), and we must not be surprised at seeing his performing acts which show indomitable courage and perseverance whenever it concerns the vindication of some holy cause of humanity. We find him exerting himself in a variety of ways to attain his objects of benevolence, and in each of them he displays a kind of energy which very few possess. Of Sir Moses' love to the study of the Hebrew language and its literature, this College bears a striking testimony. The encouragement of industry in general is with Sir Moses a sure medium for clearing the road that might lead the indigent but honest man to secure the comfort of independence to himself, and enable him likewise to become useful to others. Many were the dangers which beset him when he set out on his missions to plead the cause of suffering humanity—the horrors of war, the terror of the plague, the raging tempests of the sea, the burning sands of the desert, and the frozen rivers, breaking up the ice under his feet. But thou, O Lord, in Thy great mercy, hast always been his trust, his shield and buckler.'

Sir Moses in front of his wife's portrait in the Gothic Library at East Cliff Lodge.

The Christian community of Ramsgate, Congregationalists, Baptists, Wesleyans and Primitive Methodists, also honoured Sir Moses (who had in 1860 founded the British Syrian Relief Fund for persecuted Christians), and so did his Christian ecclesiastics who had long-standing friendships with him, Dr. Tait (the Archbishop of Canterbury), Dean Stanley, and the Earl of Shaftesbury.

To celebrate the birthday, a huge banquet was given at the Granville Hotel by the Ramsgate Improvement Committee, while the proprietor of Granville Hall gave a dinner to three hundred sick and poor people. Dinners were organised by the Commemoration Committee for 400 people at Grave's Hotel, 150 at both Christ Church Parish Hall and at St. Lawrence, and 120 poor at St. Luke's Parish. In the evening, Ramsgate and the harbour were brilliantly illuminated. Large bonfires and a fireworks display near Sir Moses' residence completed the celebration that day.

In every synagogue in the world, special services were held in honour of Sir Moses and addresses from all parts of the world praised his life and the achievements of his missions in the East, Russia, Morocco and Roumania. The local and international dimensions were captured in two inscriptions; one on the front of Ramsgate Town Hall, a large gas-lit sign invoking 'God Bless Sir Moses Montefiore: Think and Thank'; the other, engraved in Italian on a medal from the Corfu Jewish community, for Sir Moses' centenary: 'Perfect synthesis of Judaism'.

He was also honoured by the City of London with a deputation, an address and a bouquet with the inscription 'Jerusalem' in gold letters. He shook hands with all the members of the deputation and, according to Dr. Loewe:

> *'One member of the Common Council said he was eighty. ''Is that all?'' exclaimed Sir Moses, and then he gravely added, ''You have much work before you, Sir.'' '*

Through the press, Sir Moses conveyed his thanks to all those who had sent congratulations and had visited him:

> *'Grateful to Providence for the merciful protection vouchsafed to me during my long life, I rejoice in the reflection that any feeble efforts I may have made to advance the happiness and welfare of my fellow-creatures have been so kindly judged. With a fervent prayer for the health and long life of our gracious Queen, whose beneficent sway over this great and free country has caused so much happiness to all classes of her subjects, reiterating my thanks to my numerous friends, and acknowledging your courteous and flattering remarks, I have the honour to remain, yours faithfully, Moses Montefiore.'*

Throughout December 1883, more presents, letters, books and poems arrived, and charitable institutions were established (in towns in Europe, America and Australia) bearing his name. The 'Chovavey Zion' society of Warsaw celebrated the centenary at a general meeting of their members and began a 'Sir Moses Montefiore Institution' with the aim of land cultivation in

Ramsgate at the time of the Celebrations (Illustrated London News).

119

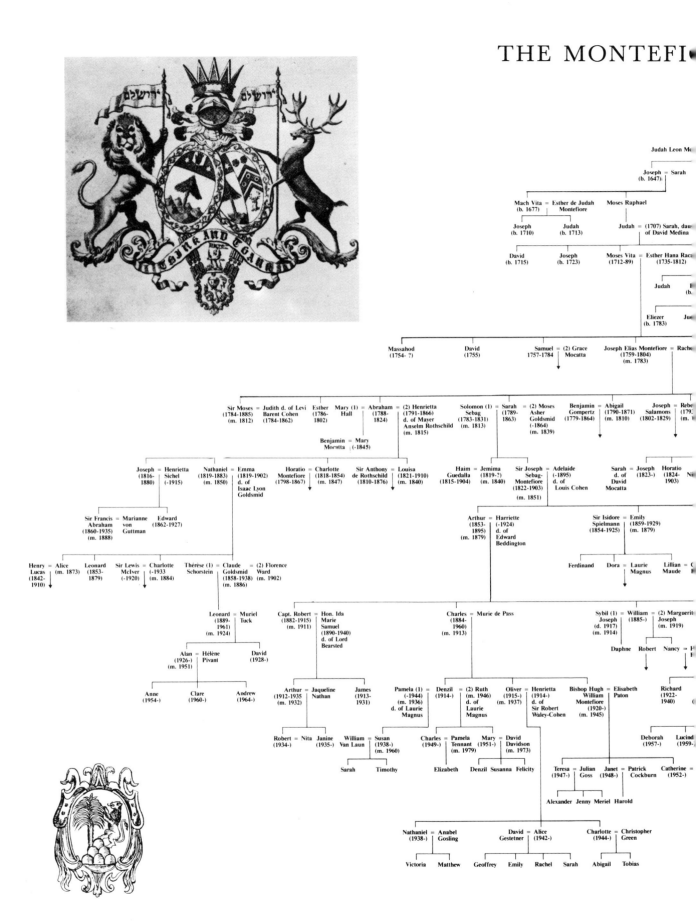

FAMILY TREE

This chart which shows the members of the family from 1605 to the present day is reproduced from an original kindly supplied by the Jewish Historical Society of England.
It is adapted from the family tree given in the Encyclopedia Judaica and another in 'The Cousinhood' by C. Bermant (Eyre and Spottiswoode 1971) partially brought up to date by S. W. Massil 1984.

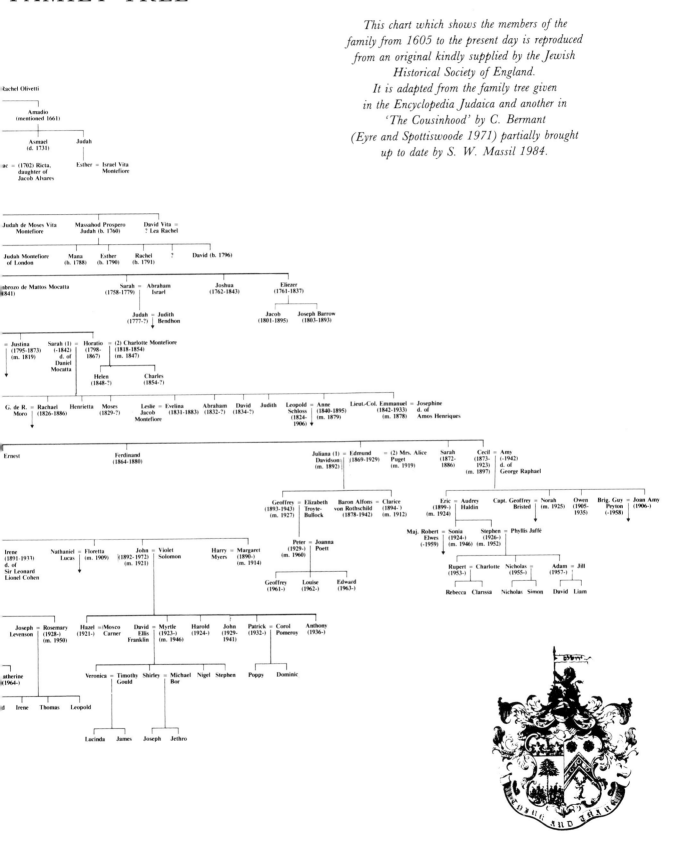

Rachel Olivetti

Amadio (mentioned 1661)

Asmael (d. 1731) — Judah

...ac = (1702) Ricta, daughter of Jacob Alvares

Esther = Israel Vita Montefiore

Judah de Moses Vita Montefiore — Massahod Prospero Judah (b. 1760) — David Vita = ? Lea Rachel

Judah Montefiore of London — Mana (b. 1788) — Esther (b. 1790) — Rachel (b. 1791) — ? — David (b. 1796)

...mbrozo de Mattos Mocatta (...841) — Sarah (1758-1779) = Abraham Israel — Joshua (1762-1843) — Eliezer (1761-1837)

Judah (1777-?) = Judith Bendhon

Jacob (1801-1895) — Joseph Barrow (1803-1893)

= Justina (1795-1873) (m. 1819) — Sarah (1) (-1842) d. of Daniel Mocatta = Horatio (1798-1867) = (2) Charlotte Montefiore (1818-1854) (m. 1847)

Helen (1848-?) — Charles (1854-?)

G. de R. Moro = Rachel (1826-1886) — Henrietta — Moses (1829-?) — Leslie = Evelina Jacob Montefiore (1831-1883) — Abraham (1832-?) — David (1834-?) — Judith — Leopold Schloss (1824-1906) = Anne (1840-1895) (m. 1879) — Lieut.-Col. Emmanuel (1842-1933) (m. 1878) = Josephine d. of Amos Henriques

Ernest — Ferdinand (1864-1880) — Juliana (1) (m. 1892) = Edmund (1869-1929) = (2) Mrs. Alice Puget (m. 1919) — Sarah (1872-1886) — Cecil (1873-1923) (m. 1897) = Amy (-1942) d. of George Raphael

Geoffrey (1893-1943) (m. 1927) = Elizabeth Troyte-Bullock — Baron Alfons von Rothschild (1878-1942) = Clarice (1894-) (m. 1912) — Eric (1899-) (m. 1924) = Audrey Haldin — Capt. Geoffrey Bristed = Norah (m. 1925) — Owen (1905-1935) — Brig. Guy Peyton (-1958) = Joan Amy (1906-)

Irene (1891-1933) d. of Sir Leonard Lionel Cohen — Nathaniel Lucas = Floretta (m. 1909) — John (1892-1972) (m. 1921) = Violet Solomon — Harry = Margaret Myers (1890-) (m. 1914)

Peter (1929-) (m. 1960) = Joanna Poett

Maj. Robert Elwes (-1959) = Sonia (1924-) (m. 1946) — Stephen (1926-) (m. 1952) = Phyllis Jaffé

Joseph Levenson = Rosemary (1928-) (m. 1950) — Hazel (1921-) = Mosco Carner — David Ellis Franklin = Myrtle (1923-) (m. 1946) — Harold (1924-) — John (1929-1941) — Patrick (1932-) = Corol Pomeroy — Anthony (1936-)

Geoffrey (1961-) — Louise (1962-) — Edward (1963-)

Rupert (1953-) = Charlotte — Nicholas (1955-) = — Adam (1957-) = Jill

Rebecca Clarissa — Nicholas Simon — David Liam

...atherine (1964-)

...d — Irene — Thomas — Leopold

Veronica = Timothy Gould — Shirley = Michael Bor — Nigel — Stephen — Poppy — Dominic

Lucinda James — Joseph Jethro

Palestine; and in Pratt Country, Kansas, U.S.A., the 'Montefiore' refugee colony expressed their gratitude for his work and sent him products from their colony.

'Sir Moses Montefiore Memorial Committees' were formed in many parts of the world in 1884. London's Lord Mayor had arranged a meeting in the Egyptian Hall at the Mansion House for 22 January to consider the celebrations for the following October, but Sir Moses requested that this be cancelled. Nevertheless, preparations went ahead in synagogues, charitable institutions and schools. Two nephews of Sir Moses, Arthur Cohen and Joseph Sebag (president and vice-president of the Board of Deputies), took a leading part in organising the functions in honour of the hundredth birthday.

In 1884 the Conference at Kattowice of the Russian 'Lovers of Zion' opened its proceedings with a special prayer for Sir Moses. The synagogues in England held special services, and in London, Dr. Hermann Adler delivered a magnificent sermon at the Bevis Marks synagogue, which was inspirational:

> 'I claim it as an event without parallel in the annals of Judaism that this same festival service is being held simultaneously, the same psalms being sung, the same prayers being offered up, not merely in cities far off which own the sway of our gracious Queen, but in the greater number of Hebrew congregations throughout the world. The love and veneration which centre in the name of Sir Moses Montefiore are due, it seems to me, to the fact that he realizes within himself some of the best and noblest traits of the true Israelite. At each journey he undertook, some cruel law was abolished in deference to him, and as he went forth, with no protection save the dignity of his silver hairs, half-savage countries submitted themselves to his spirit of compassion, and learned justice and mercy from his lips. And even when, despite his strenuous efforts, he did not attain all that was desired, he yet succeeded in wiping out some grievous prejudice, silenced some cruel slander, taught the ignorant multitude a better conception of his religion and his race. But his sympathies are not confined to the claims of his country, nor are his affections determined by his race and faith. (Yet) Is not a Montefiore esteemed the more because he is not ashamed to declare and manifest before the world his allegiance to his faith? He gladly declares that for the last seventy-two years since he entered upon the holy estate of matrimony his Sabbath lamp has ever been kindled; whether tossing on the wave of the ocean, or encamped in the Syrian desert. Oh, that we all would grasp the best and noblest characteristics of the life we honour this day, that we may determine to show by our life, that "fervent Judaism and patriotic citizenship are absolutely consistent with one another!" '

Sir Moses had enjoyed a close friendship with the Ashkenazi Chief Rabbi, Nathan Marcus Adler, had welcomed him on his arrival at Dover in July 1844, and been present the next day when Adler was in the Great Synagogue in London. Forty years later, his son Hermann Adler delivered this paean to Sir Moses. Six hundred poor people were given a dinner by the Bevis Marks congregation, the Jewish Working Men's Club held a celebration and Jewish schools received presents for the pupils. Sir Moses gave £100 each to Sephardi and Ashkenazi communities, to the Mansion House Poor Box and to each of the four Holy Cities in the Holy Land. Adler also delivered his special service at Hereson at 1.30 p.m. Sir Moses was propped up by pillows in his four-poster double bed, from which hung the Hebrew inscription 'If I forget thee, O Jerusalem, let my right hand forget her cunning', and around which were pictures of the Queen and Royal family, scenes from the Holy Land, and a tablet with the inscription of the Decalogue. The Chief Rabbi recited the prayer previously given in the synagogue and Sir Moses was greeted by representatives of the Anglo–Jewish community and a scribe from Wilna, who

Photographic portrait of Sir Moses on entering his 100th year 1883. (Royal Archives, Windsor Castle.)

had brought him the Pentateuch scroll.

The image of the centenarian had not altered much in the intervening years since Orientalist, Professor Max Miller, at Ramsgate remarked in 1871:

> *'Now, sitting in the Tabernacle at the table with Sir Moses Montefiore, I can fancy myself in the presence of the Patriarch Abraham, sitting in his tent, where his hospitality was accepted by angels, and gladdened the heart of all comers.'*

Ramsgate's festivities had begun with free coal delivered to the poor and the distribution of one hundred pairs of blankets to the poor by the local mayor at the Town Hall. Printed on each blanket were the words 'Think and Thank'. Almost every street was decorated and flags were hung across the streets. In the harbour the ships were similarly bedecked. Huge crowds arrived from neighbouring towns and villages to witness the scene and read the banners stretched across the streets proclaiming 'The man whom the people delight to honour' and 'Europe claims his birth, all nations own his worth'. As in 1883 a procession marched from one end of the town to the other with bands and banners. It included the mayors and officials of neighbouring towns and villages, the mayor of Ramsgate, the deputy-mayor, the aldermen and town councillors, and the travelling carriage (in which Sir Moses and his wife rode in Russia, Poland, France and Italy) drawn by six horses.

East Cliff Lodge, Ramsgate.

After the special service at 1.30 p.m., at which the Delegate Chief Rabbi recited the prayer composed by his father, the Rev. Dr. N. M. Adler, the visitors were introduced to Sir Moses. Dr. Loewe depicted the scene in the room:

A portrait of Sir Moses aged 100.

'It is a strange and fascinating picture! There, in the right-hand corner of a large high-backed, old-fashioned chintz sofa sits a patriarchal figure supported by pillows. This impressive picture of age, tended by love and respect, is lighted from the right by a stream of sunshine, which pours through the upper panes of a large angular bay window, and rests gently upon a grand head, full of character, fringed with a short, closely-cut, snow-white beard. One hand of Sir Moses is thrown negligently across a tall arm of the sofa, the other rests upon the ample skirts of a purple silk dressing gown. Close to the head of the sofa stands a table covered with baskets and great bouquets of flowers. Around on the walls are pictures of the Queen and the Royal family, and of scenes in the Holy Land, and a beautifully carved tablet with the inscription of the Decalogue over a standing desk, for the use of the reader when reciting the daily prayers; also a palm branch and a citron, over which he pronounced the blessings at the Feast of Tabernacles.'

The prayer which the Delegate Chief Rabbi had offered in the synagogue was now recited. Sir Moses stood during most of the recitation, and fervently joined in the prayer for the Queen. Afterwards he thanked the representatives from the Anglo–Jewish community who were introduced to him, and met Rabbi Zvi Hirsch Volozin, who had written twenty-four scrolls of the Torah by Sir Moses' request over the years for distribution to specific synagogues. The rabbi had brought the Pentateuch scroll. Sir Moses was elated. At two o'clock the procession from the town hall reached East Cliff and a deputation visited the Lodge so that Sir Moses could invest the new first mayor of Ramsgate, Mr. Kennett, with his present of a new gold chain of office. He also met the members of the Commemoration Committee, after which the vicar of Ramsgate read an address to Sir Moses.

Evening prayers took place in the synagogue, after which the visitors proceeded to Judith, Lady Montefiore Theological College where Dr. Loewe, the Principal, held a special service, with a prayer for the life of Sir Moses, the essence of which was that the latter's name had uplifted Judaism in self-respect and self-confidence. A public banquet for residents of Ramsgate and Sir Moses' relatives and friends then ensued at St. George's Hall with the mayor presiding. A message arrived from Sir Moses during the dinner:

'Sir Moses wishes to send a message of friendly greeting to the Mayor of Ramsgate and to his guests assembled this evening. He desires to drink a glass of wine with them, and wished good health and prosperity to them and to the town. He regrets much that he is unable to be present with them tonight.'

During the evening, a torch-light procession began at the Town Hall and marched to East Cliff, where another grand display of fireworks took place. The whole town was illuminated that night. The day was epitomised in Queen Victoria's telegram to Sir Moses:

'I wish to renew my sincere congratulations to you on this day which marks your completion of a century of loyalty and philanthropy.'

From East Cliff Lodge Sir Moses thanked everyone for celebrating his centenary, above all the Board of the London Committee of Deputies of British Jews. To the Board he wrote:

'My heart is overflowing with thankfulness to the Most High for having tended me all my life unto this day. My gratitude to the distinguished members of your Board, with whom it has been my privilege to be associated in their unceasing endeavours to promote the interests of the communities at home and abroad for so long a period. I appreciate highly the renewed assurance of friendship by which you have greatly honoured me, and earnestly pray that the Most Supreme may shield and protect you and your families, so as to enable you to continue your noble exertions in the cause of our holy religion, in the cause of suffering humanity, and in the vindication of truth and justice.'

It was indicative of Sir Moses' loyalty to Queen and country as well as his own religion that his last activities included a celebration of the Queen's birthday. He gave orders to provide a dinner for the poor at Ramsgate and tea for the teachers and pupils of the Jews' Infant School in London. His last public act was to send a massive silver tea and coffee set to Princess Beatrice as a wedding present on 17 July.

The telegram from the Queen from Osborn House on the engagement of her daughter Princess Beatrice.

125

Sir Moses Montefiore died on 28 July 1885. The Lord Mayor of London spoke of him as 'the most distinguished citizen of London'. The Court of Common Council put on record that Sir Moses had left behind him a memory 'which will be long cherished in many lands'. The funeral was held on Friday, 31 July. Memorial services were held in synagogues and churches, and alluded to the principles he had advanced and practised. His body was taken to his synagogue and then to the mausoleum, where a lamp was suspended from the cupola with a Hebrew inscription 'The soul of man is the light of God'. As requested by Sir Moses in his will:

The exterior of the Mausoleum at Ramsgate showing the granite pillar presented to Sir Moses by the Governor of Jerusalem.

'I desire that my remains may rest by the side of those of my beloved wife in the mausoleum near our Synagogue at Hereson, and that my funeral may be as private as may be.'

He left most of his worldly possessions to specific Jewish organisations. On the tombstone was the inscription

'In memory of Sir Moses Montefiore, Bart, F.R.S., of East Cliff Lodge, Ramsgate. Born the 8th Heshván 5545 A.M. Died the 16th of Menákhem Ab. 5645 = 28th July 1885. In the hundred and first year of his age. "I have set the Lord always before me".'

At the end of Dr. Loewe's 741 page analysis of Sir Moses' life, completed nearly one hundred years' ago, he concluded with an assessment that has stood the scrutiny of subsequent historians. Sir Moses, he estimated, had 'fought so sturdily in youth the battle of life, and . . . afterwards devoted himself with

Sir Moses' tomb.

such unwearying ardour to the task of combating hatred, persecution, and fanaticism, of severing the bonds of physical and moral slavery, and of aiding in the establishment of religious toleration all over the world. His unparalleled devotion to the sacred cause of humanity in general, and the unclouded halo of a spotless integrity which encircles his name, will ever afford a splendid example for emulation no less than the dauntless courage with which he set to work for the rescue of the suffering and the oppressed.' A poem in *The Jewish Chronicle* was the final tribute:

We do not weep; we have few tears,
Although our thoughts are softly blended
With tenderness for him, whose years
Have nobly, and how gently ended:
We do not weep. What tears avail
To hold him back, to fan the flicker
Of waning life, of days that fail?
The father's summons cometh quicker!

So, like a tired child he went,
More than one wearied with the history
Of all those hundred years, and bent
Towards the first; the last great mystery.
Straight towards the light, leaving the dark
Of death, crowned with goodly measure
Of age extreme, our Patriarch
Sought, and has won eternal treasure

For youth is fleeting, fleeting too
Is sordid gain, but such Heaven blesses
As him, the noble leader, who
Strove in fair fight for his successes,
Against tyrannic force, and now he lies,
He lies at rest, his mission finished
With peace sealed on his tranquil brow
Content, at tyranny diminished!

Then brush the startling tears away,
We dare not mourn for him, thus lying;
So calmly in the summer day,
We may not mar his rest by crying,
The long, long years are full of deeds
To pillow soft, that grand head hoary
And God has ministered to his needs,
And traced the last word on the story.

INDEX